Creativity And Self Expression
A Journey

By Gina Bronzini Ahrens

Photography used with permission from Theresa Le and Rebecca Ahrens.

Photography and design by:

    Theresa Le http://www.theresalephotography.com/
    Rebecca E. Ahrens https://www.linkedin.com/in/rebeccaeahrens
    Gina B. Ahrens

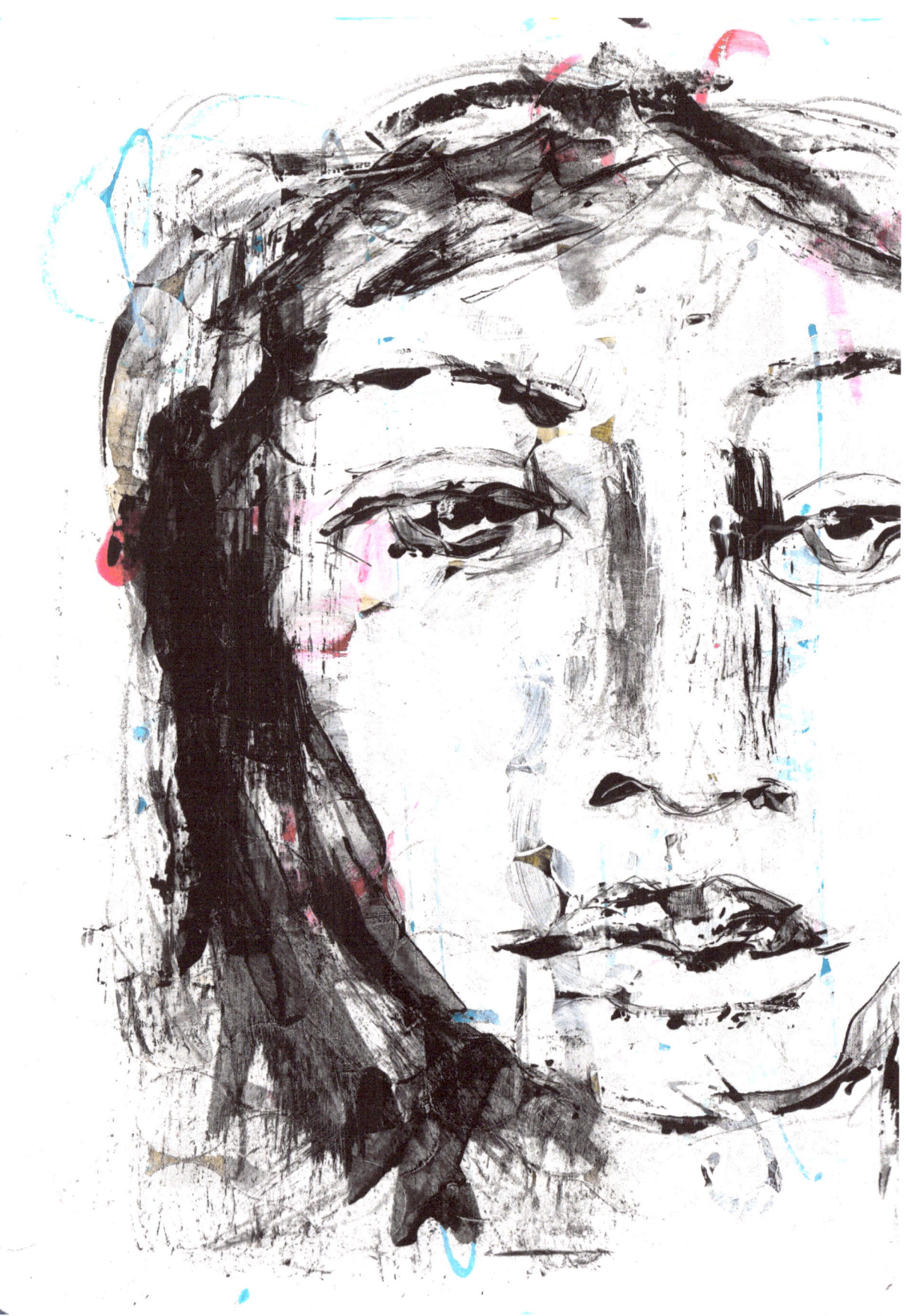

Acknowledgements:

I wish to give special, and very large, thanks to all who have helped me get this far on my life's journey. Most especially to my fabulous husband, Robert, and daughter, Rebecca, without whom none of this would have been possible. Without their never ending love and support I would never have had the courage to do this. I love you guys!

Thank you to my parents, Kathy and Albert Bronzini, for birthing me, and to friends and family for supporting me. Thank you to all the wonderful teachers I have had over the years. You all have taught me so much and I am forever indebted to all of you.

Big thanks to my brainstorming editing team for putting up with me and my crazy ramblings. These ladies kept me sane and on task which is a huge feat. I know very well I drive everyone crazy on a good day. So huge thanks to Annette Bronzini, Elizabeth Bronzini, Theresa le, Cindy Utter and Nancy Young.

Introduction:

First, let me say welcome. This book is a little peek into my head, how I work and what I think. I am by no means a licensed counselor or other professional. The steps and questions outlined in this book are what work for me. They are questions I have asked, and do continue to ask, myself on my forward journal down my life's path of creativity and self expression. Please don't be afraid to ask for professional advice if you need it. We all need a helping hand now and then. There is no shame in that.

This book is intended to be a journaling workbook, filled with thought provoking prompts from which you can, maybe, glean some insight into yourself and who you are.

I hope it helps you figure out your journey of art and creativity, and how to get there. This isn't a technique book on how to do this or that. It is a thought provoking journey intended upon teaching you how to set your creative soul free. How to play in the sunlight without fear, but with nothing but joyful exuberance.

I, personally, find the lessons here helpful and I hope you do to. Life's path to art and self expression may be bumpy and messy, but I hope to help you shine some light on it so you can at least view your destination.

www.ginabahrens.com

Twitter: @ginabahrens

Instagram: https://www.instagram.com/ginabahrens/

Pinterest: https://www.pinterest.com/GinaBAhrens/

YouTube: https://www.youtube.com/user/ginabahrens

Table Of Contents:

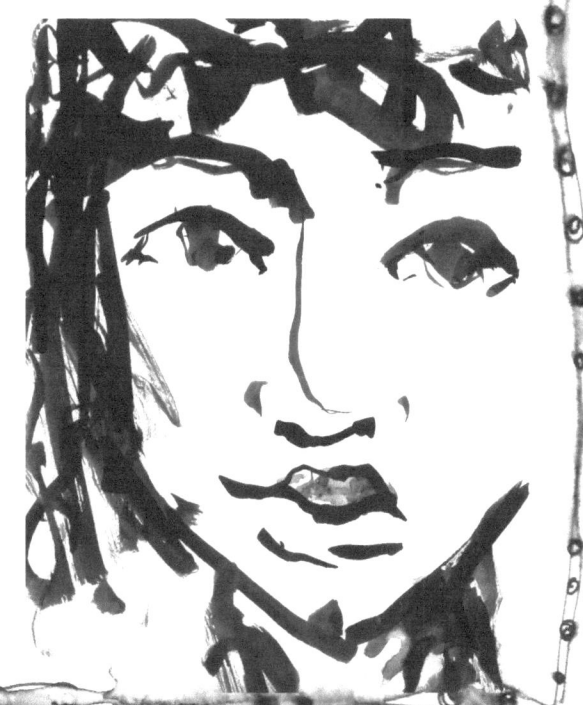

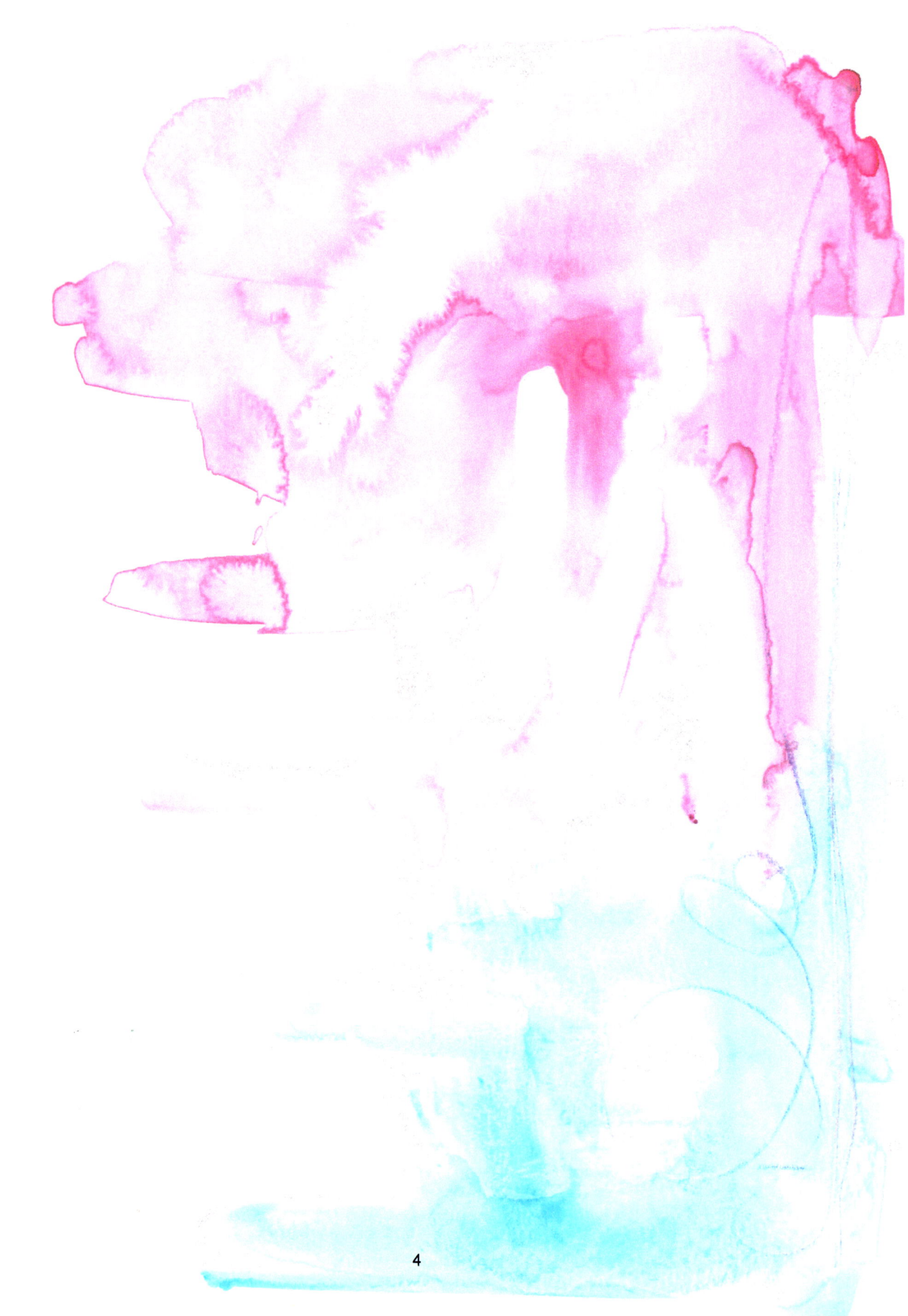

4

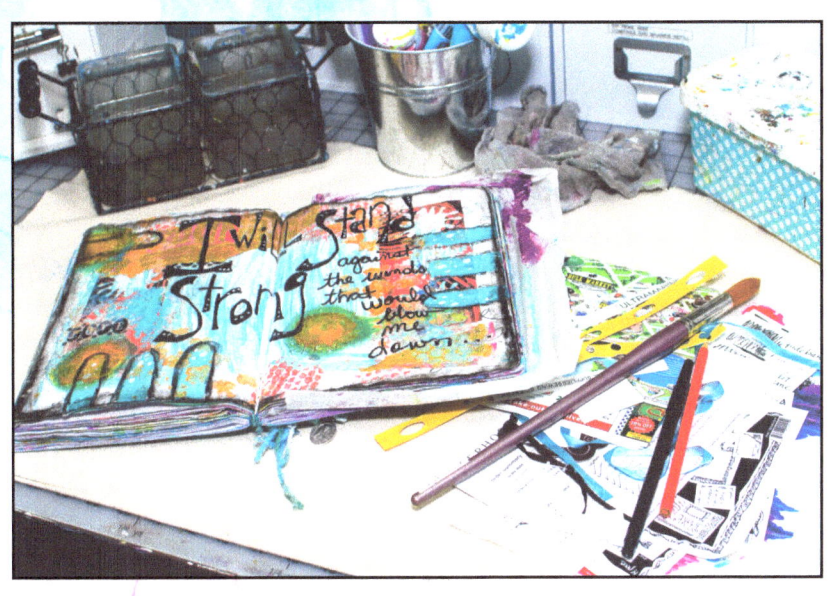

Living A Creative Life:

"Life is a journey that should be enjoyed. To continue to be creative we must move forward. Creativity feeds the soul, but must be nurtured. A creative life is not always easy. It can be challenging and stressful. The rewards from those challenges can be enormous. To continue we must move forward in the bright light of our own fabulous journey. So take the ride of your life on its forward path and enjoy the view. You won't regret it...and anyway...what have you got to lose!"

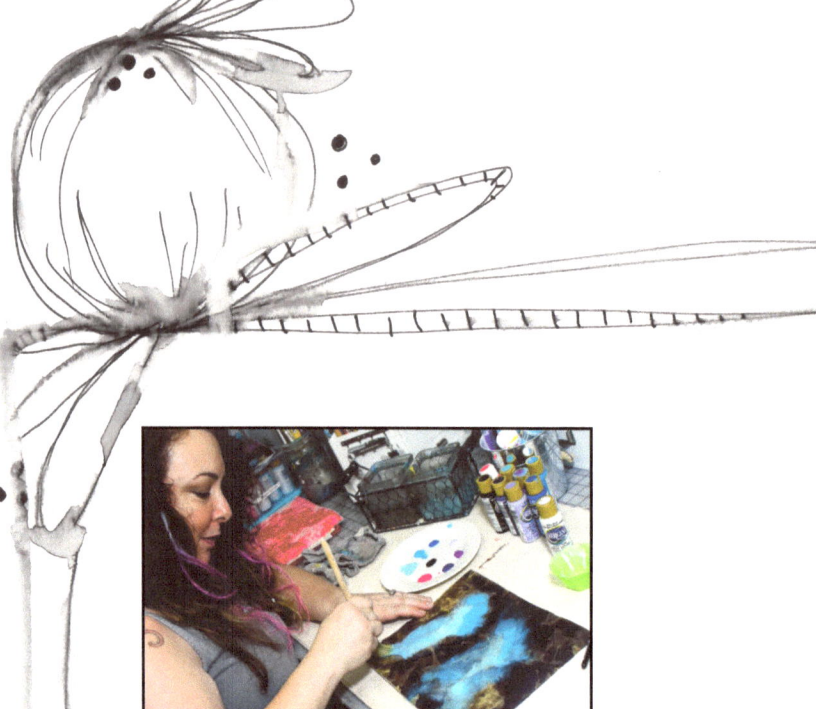

What are you doing creatively today? Some days I don't feel like arting (I know...shocker) but it happens. Then I clean the studio room, reorganize, sort and stuff. This helps me find my calm place that I can create from and...bonus...I usually find things I forgot I had. I am by no means an expert. This is just what I do.

We all have moments when our muse, or inner creative soul, is mute. We can't bribe her enough to start talking. So go forward and get out of your normal routine. Do something different until you wake up that creative spark.

Being creative is not always about getting out the paints and brushes, but opening yourself up to the different possibilities in the world around you. Get out of the house once in a while, take a walk, take some inspiration pictures or tour a museum. All of these things will fuel your creative soul.

What are you doing to fuel your creative soul today? What can you do to wake up your muse and get her talking?

Journal or create a page prompted by the statements on the previous page.

What can you do to feed your muse and keep her happy?

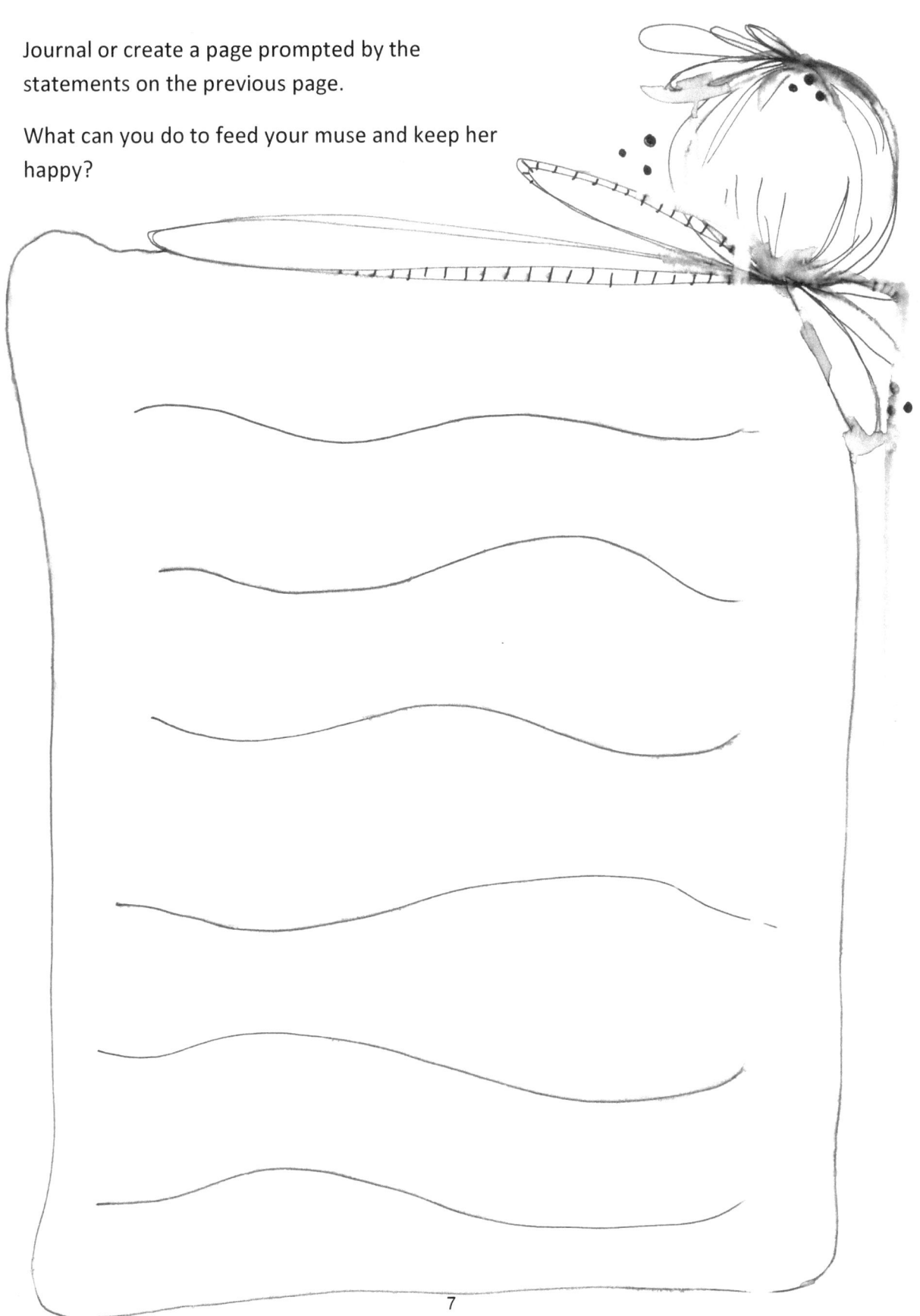

In my opinion, being creative is not something that is a matter of talent, but a state of mind. It is something you strive to achieve and therefore practice. The saying "Nothing good ever comes easy" keeps coming to mind. Finding your true voice, or creative side, takes time and a lot of practice. There is no shortcut. You must always strive to try new things, to be willing to fail and keep going. Just make sure you remember to enjoy the journey along the way.

Your creative life doesn't have to be about anything more than doing what makes you happy. Does your art make you happy? If so, cool! Put a gag on that inner negative voice. I, myself, have created some truly ugly art. I still have most of it. It is part of my journey and therefore important. Remember, we all have to start somewhere. We do not come out of the womb drawing and painting like a master. A creative life should be a joyful and expressive journey. We have the opportunity along the way to learn, grow and stretch our creative wings. Take advantage of those opportunities and enjoy the journey.

A life of art and self expression is not all about happy times and successes, but also failures. Sometimes we learn the most from those failures or "happy accidents". I strive to fail.

Living a creative life requires one basic rule: honesty with ones self. Being open and honest with yourself, above all others, is the most important thing you can do and the hardest.

Doing this, though, will bring some earthy, gritty feeling and some realism to your art. No one has to get it but you. We are here first and foremost to get in touch with our inner creative selves, to be honest with said self and allow that inner person to express themselves in a healthy creative way.

So go out today and get real with yourself, if no one else. What do you want? What do you feel? And, express that in your art.

Express here, with art or words, who you really are and who you wish to be. How will you get there?

Get real with yourself and express it here.

Sometimes the best thing you can do for yourself and your creative soul is to get out of your own way. Sometimes the thing holding us back the most is ourselves. My question to you: how do we quash that and move forward?

This process can be difficult at best. I have a tendency to either jump in without thinking or rush forward without considering the consequences. I also tend to hide and do nothing. The negative side of me never seems to shut the hell up although, sometimes she is quieter and has less to say. I think we need to learn to live with the inner critic rather than silence her. She tends to tell me now that "You know you can do better" rather than "You suck and are untalented." However, she is still there and I am learning to embrace her and value her opinion.

As my Grandmother would say to you "Nothing good in life ever came easy." So if getting your creative life off the ground seems hard don't be discouraged. A life worth living is a life hard won.

What can you do to get out of your own way? To learn to value your inner critic and what she or he has to say?

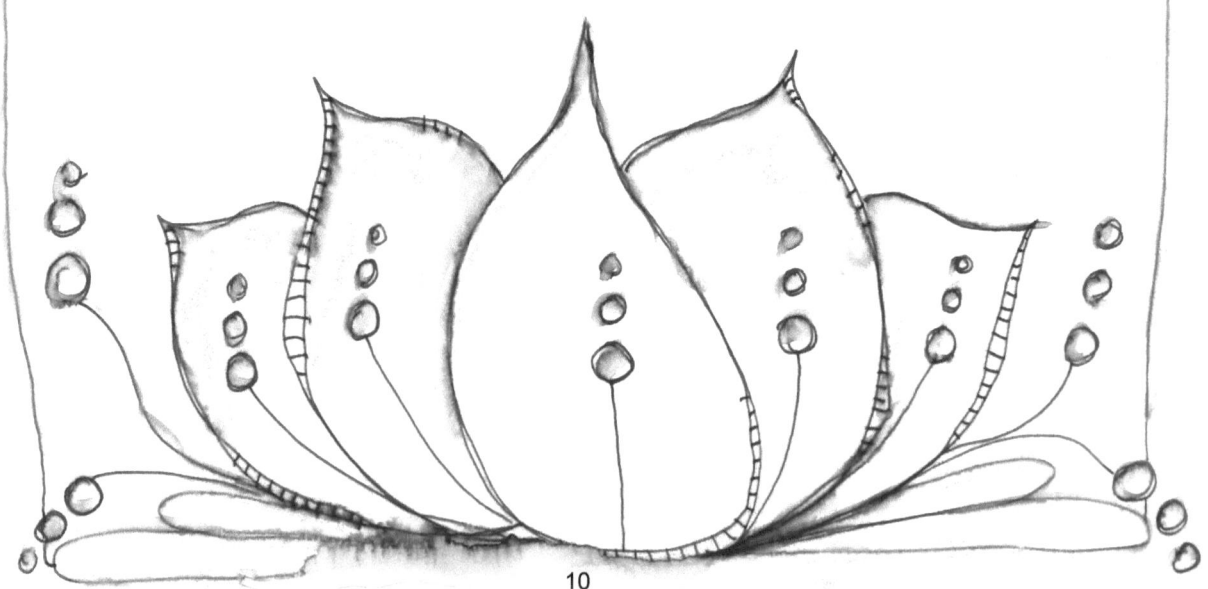

How can you erase the self doubt and move
forward in your fabulous creative light?

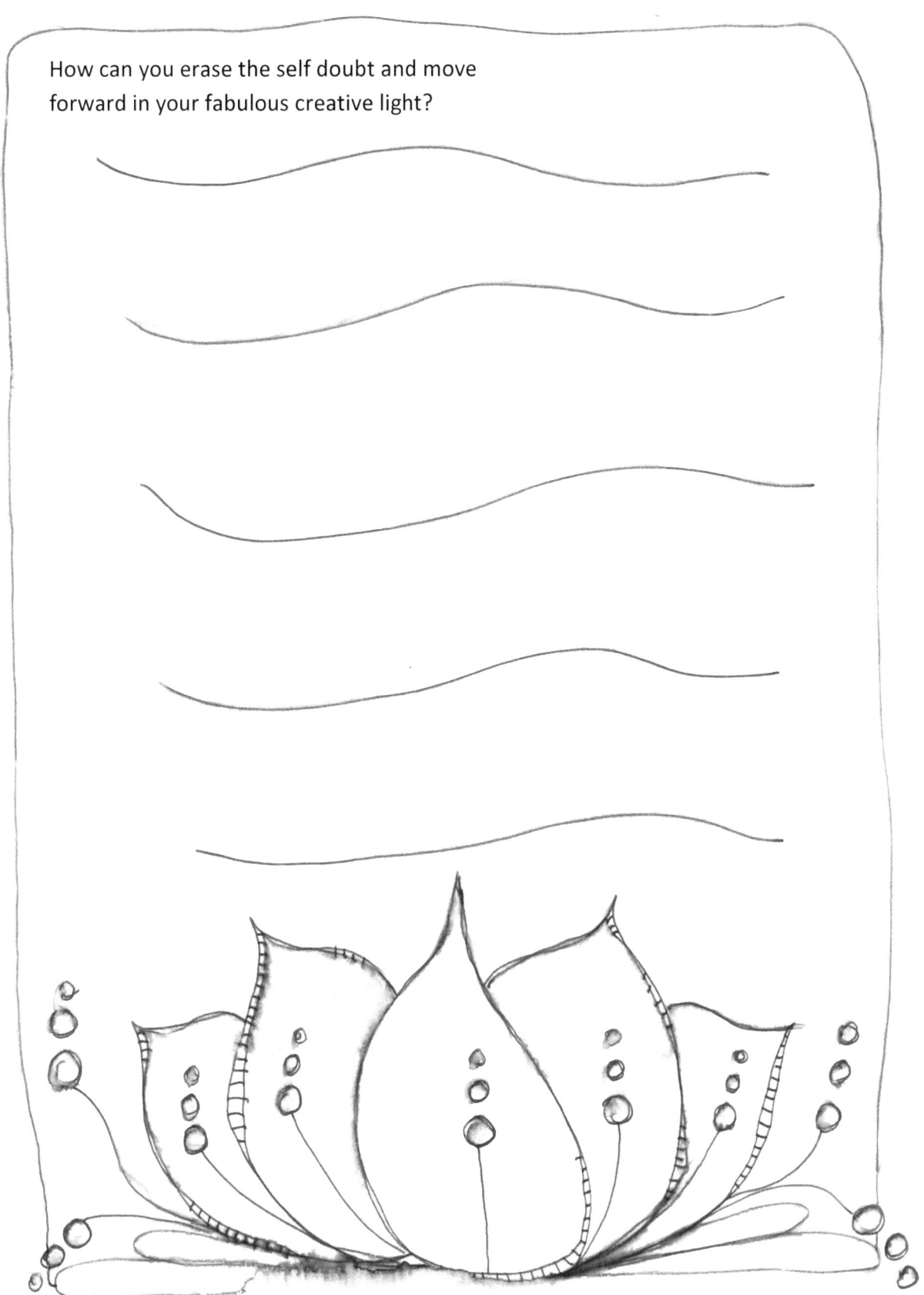

I am loving the idea of starting the day with a daily sketch, dancing at your desk to music no one but you can hear or just enjoying life...a great way to start the day. Remember to stop, relax, take a minute to de-stress. Start the day with no stress. It is a great thing to do for your mental health and well being.

So go out today and smell the roses, do a sketch, take a walk, take some deep breaths. Remember that no matter how hard or stressful things get we are still here breathing and living. As my Dad says "We are still on the right side of the dirt so it's all good."

I am celebrating love, life, and creativity. My mission in life is to encourage you all to do the same. We cannot expect every day will be happy and rosy. It makes those that are all the more worthy of celebration.

Life is a journey that should be enjoyed. To continue to be creative we must move forward. So take the ride of your creative life on its forward path and enjoy the view. Let it inspire your next bout of creativity. What have you got to loose?

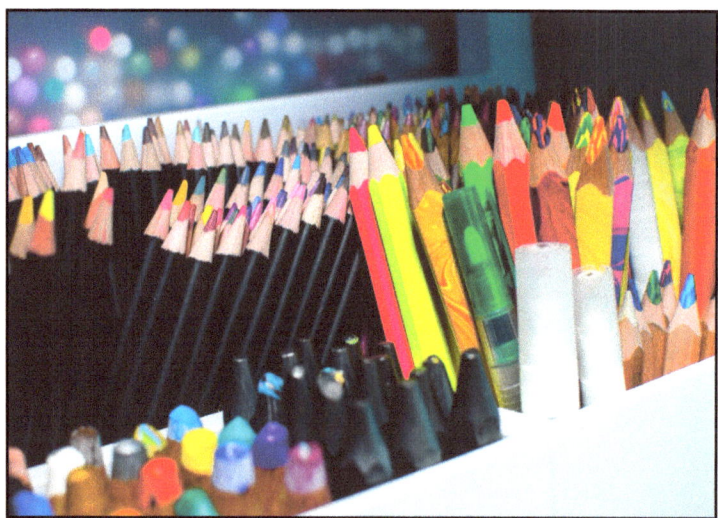

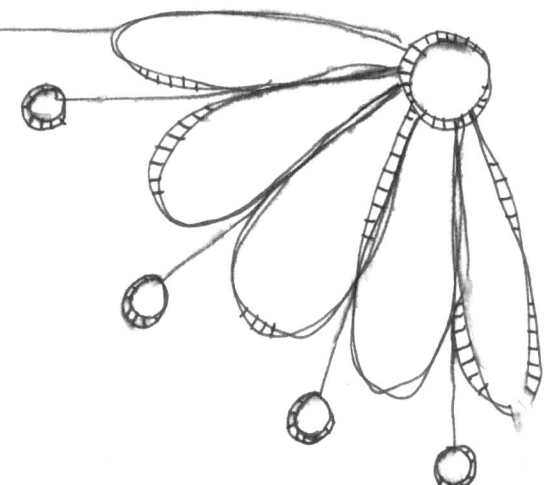

Do you want to put daily creativity into practice? How can you make it happen?

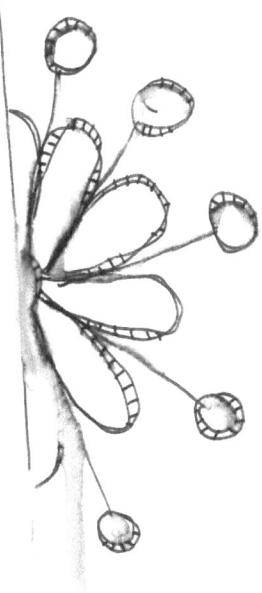

I haven't gotten much art done today. For the first time in a while the whole family is home and there are no special events or holidays. So we have spent the day cleaning, purging, doing laundry etc. Boy have we gotten a lot done. One of the things I wanted to do was do something with the mountain of shoes always by the front door as we take them off when we come in the house. We were thinking of going out to buy something and that kind of didn't sit well with me. We have so much stuff. We don't have anything we can re-purpose? After some thought and searching, we do have something that will work and solve a big problem. Life, and art, is more fun and less stressful if we can learn to roll with whatever happens. My goal is to worry less about moments of the unexpected into my art and life.

Ever have moments where you speak to the universe and say "Really?" or "Why?" ....of course you did, we all do. Those moments happen to everyone. I try not to let them stress me out any more than needed. Instead I try to say, "OK, let's do this." I try to be accepting of whatever happens, if I can, and work with it. Art has taught me this.

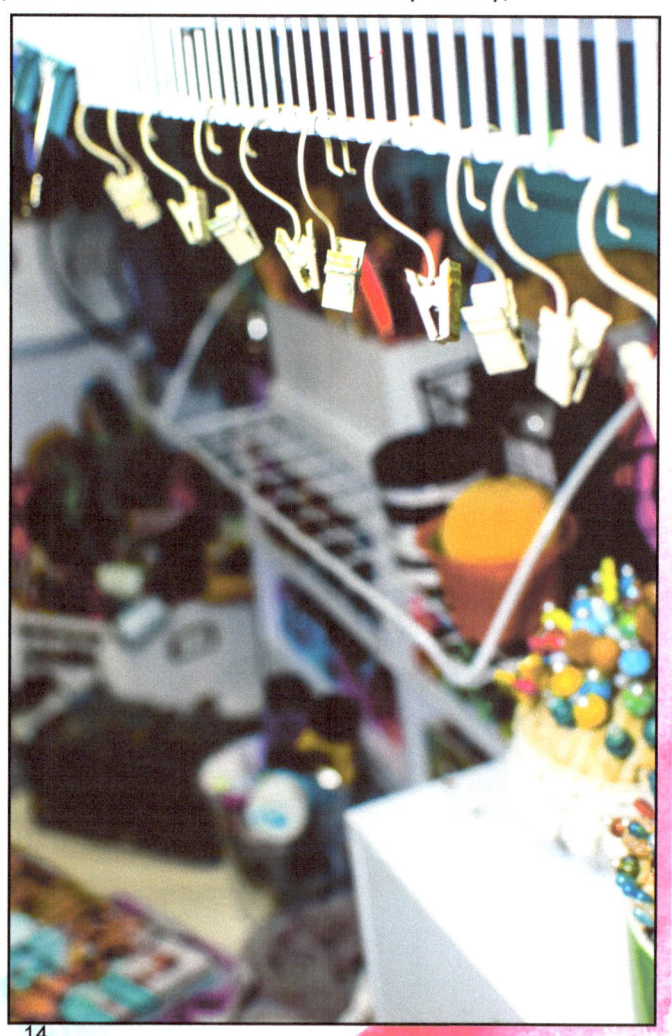

Sometimes in life and art, shit happens. You can't prevent it. You can't always prepare for it. You just need to take a deep breath and figure out how to work with it. Creativity isn't always about making pretty pictures. Sometimes it is just about rethinking a problem or situation to come up with a unique solution. Look at situations and obstacles from all angles. How can you solve them other than the obvious?

14

How can you make something fabulous out of something unexpected? Express it here.

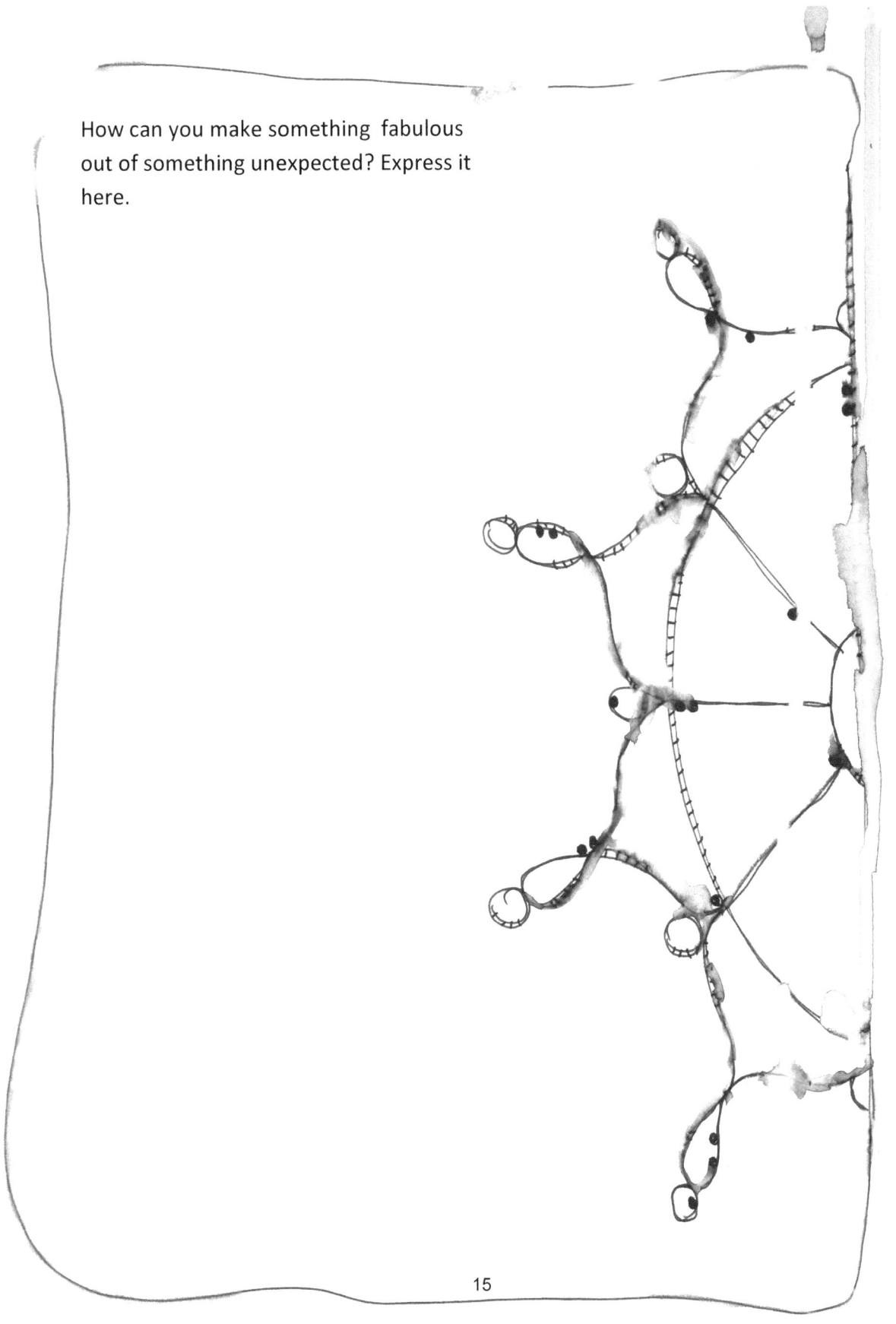

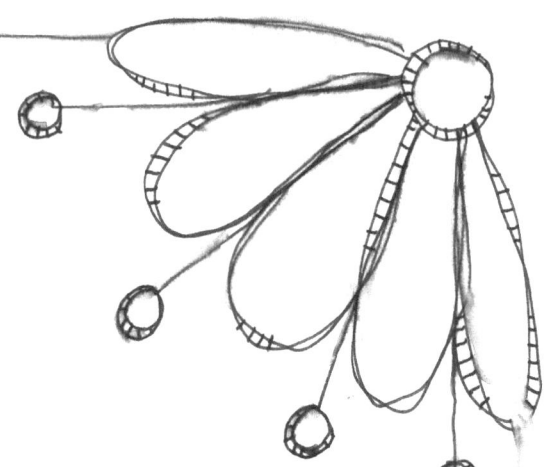

I like to be in control, but life (and creativity) is not something you can always control. Sometime things just happen. In learning to deal with the fact that I have anxiety issues, among other things, and I have to own up to the fact that I cannot control everything. Trying to control everything makes it worse rather than better. I strive to be able to go with the flow of things more when it is appropriate. Sometimes things in life come at you in a rush or a tidal wave. All you can do is hold on tight, hold your breath, if needed, and tackle one problem at a time. It won't last forever and usually craziness like this is followed by calm.

Your life, and artistic path will have moments of calm still waters in which you can just cruise and relax. It will also have crazy, hectic, sometime screwed up moments that pass by in a blur of activity. Enjoy the calm waters while you can, because another tidal wave will be coming soon enough.

How you handle these moments shows a lot about who you are and where you are headed. Remember, no matter if life is crazy busy, calm and still, or someone is throwing rocks at your head....to be mindful of your breathing, make a list and for gods sake put on a helmet....those rocks hurt.

How can you let go of control and let your creative
muse sing? Do you want to?

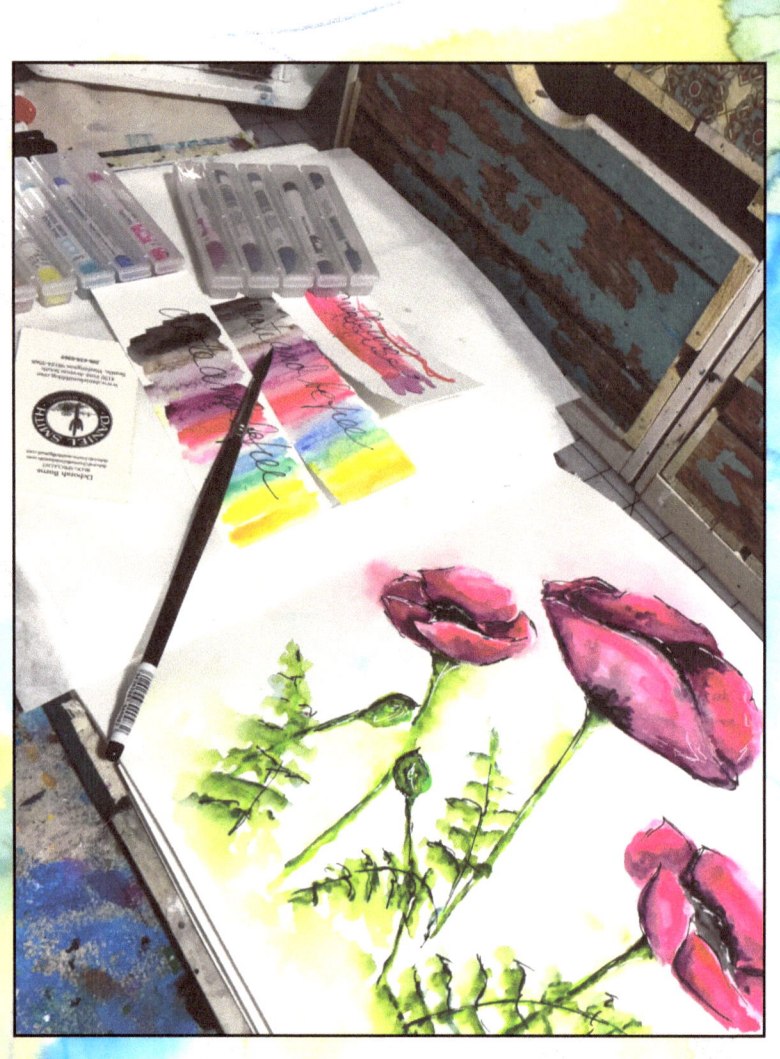

"Don't let negativity and self doubt put a road block in your life's path to happiness."

Gina B. Ahrens

Finding Your Inspiration:

"I can find inspiration anywhere. Shopping at the local market I often stop to take photos of the beautiful blooms, graffiti on the building and yes even cracks in the cement. Even in the midst of city living craziness there is beauty to be found and inspiration to be had. Open your eyes and creative soul to that which the world has to offer. You never know where it may lead you. It might be really interesting."

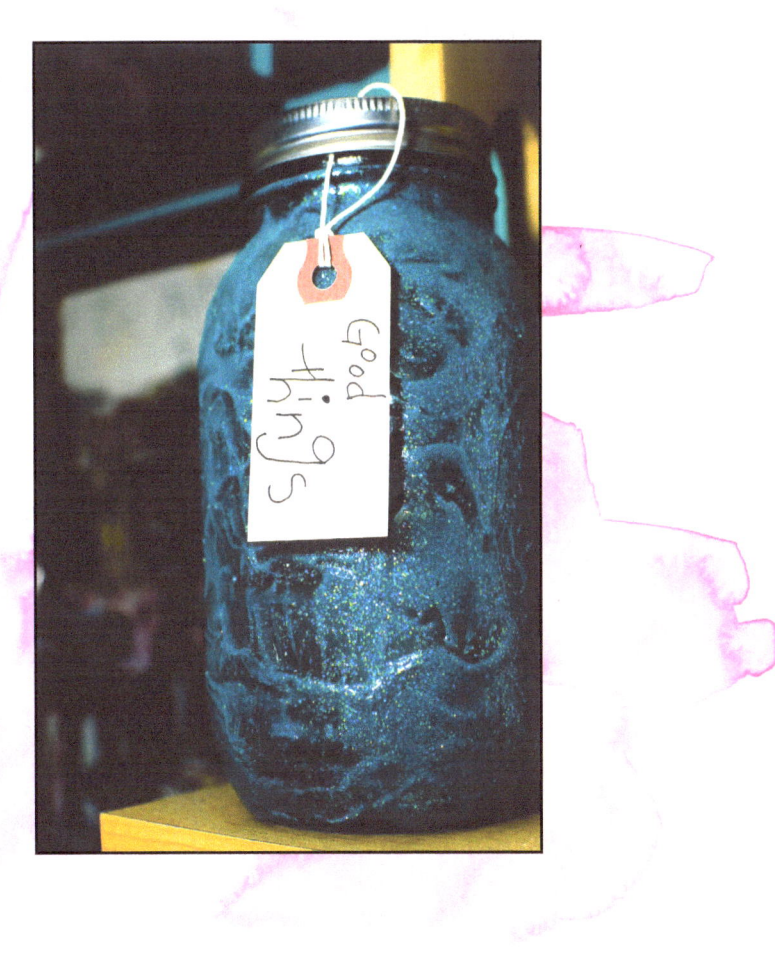

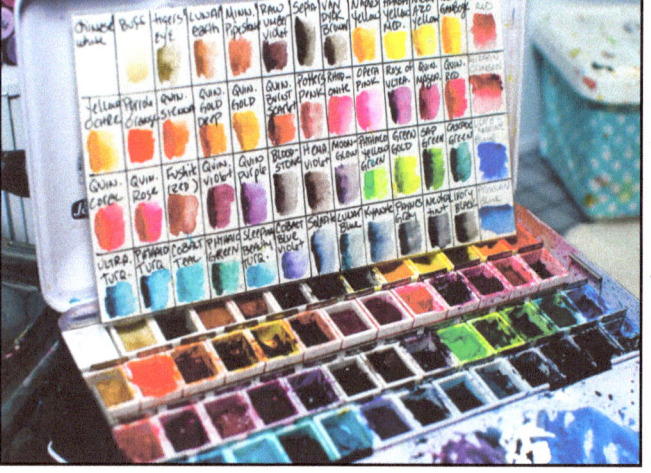

Remember to be observant of the world around you whether you are in an art class, at the museum or just at the grocery store. Inspiration for art and creativity can be found everywhere.

Living a creative life, for me at least, is about being open to those opportunities whenever they strike. It's about being present in the moment and observant of that which is around you.

Sometimes when I am stuck for inspiration, I force myself to get out of the house, go for a walk around the neighborhood or maybe have coffee with friends and, yes, even go to the gym.

I have been inspired by the pattern of cracks in the cement and the colors in the graffiti on the wall. It doesn't have to be pretty to be inspiring. These things renew my soul's purpose and help me find my direction.

What things to you do? What helps you stay the course, be creative and be determined? Where did you find your creative opportunities or inspiration today?

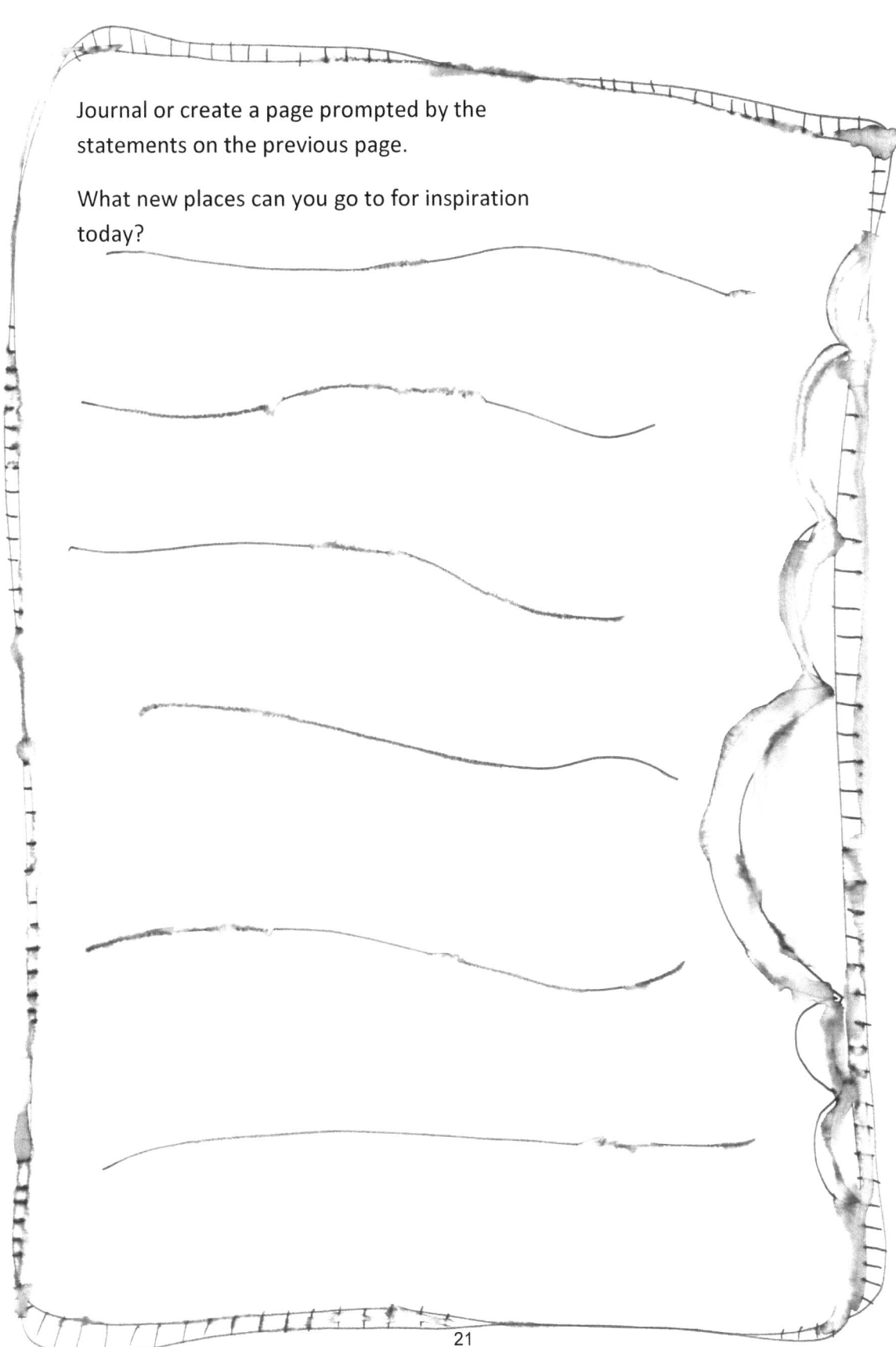

Journal or create a page prompted by the statements on the previous page.

What new places can you go to for inspiration today?

Sometimes, for me, cleaning out the cobwebs of my physical space allows me to also clear them out of my non physical space. This allows the creativity to keep flowing and the inspiration to fly in.

I woke up this morning, after cleaning and redoing parts of my kitchen and family room, to some really great ideas bouncing around in my head. They were like little kids all shouting "me first!" at the same time.

Every creative soul out there has moments of doubt, lack of inspiration or moments of artistic crisis. All artists out there go through this at some time just like we all have some times where we make ugly art, lol.

This is part of the journey, part of the learning experience and adventure. For me, I have a few things I do to get through. We shall list them here:

1. never give up

2. clean the office

3. make backgrounds

4. go for a walk

5. visit a museum or gallery

6. watch art instruction DVD's or online videos

7. read an art book

8. chat/share with art peeps

9. stop listening to negative people

10.   do some timed art exercises

Ok...so there...now my secret is out. That's all of them, I think, and not in any particular order. We all have moments of creative crisis. It can happen to the best of us. Remember that the creative process should be one that makes you happy and allows your soul to fly free. If it doesn't, then what is the point? So get out and clean out those cobwebs. Do those non creative things you have been putting off and see if that helps clear the clutter out of the way of your creative flow. I know it works for me.

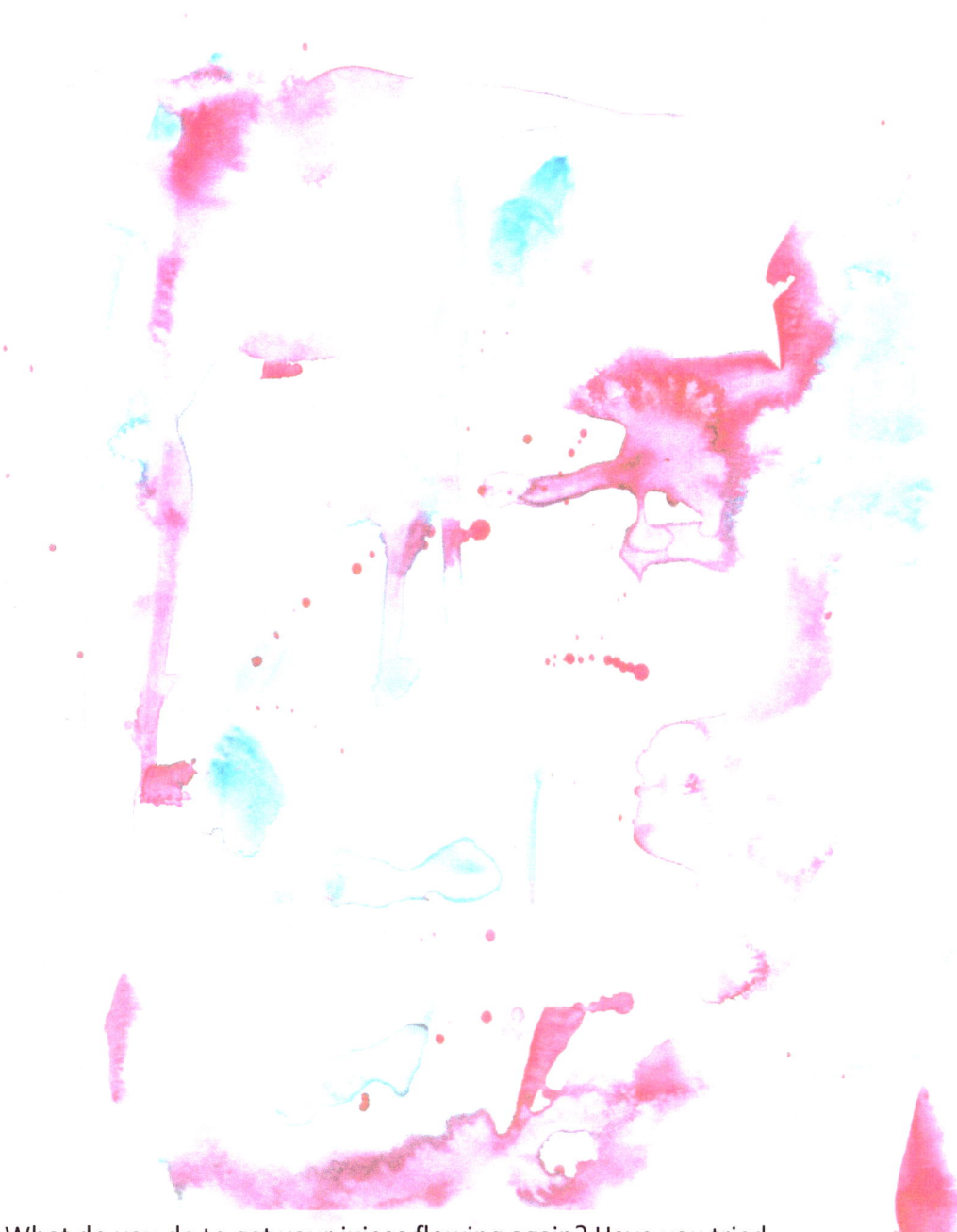

What do you do to get your juices flowing again? Have you tried unplugging for the day? Getting out of the house?

Express here what you can do to get those inspirational juices flowing again.

Ever go to the art store to just look around but don't buy anything even though you have money? Go to the library but never check out a book? I have done this many times and in the process met some fabulously creative souls.

Just the act of getting out of the house, walking around and chatting with people, helps stimulate the creative flow. Today I was chatting about art stuff with the people at the office supply store when I was picking up an order. The guy had a knitting question and then also had an art question.

You never know where you are going to meet an interesting soul, get a creative spark or help someone else with their creative endeavors. Sharing of yourself should be part of life's journey. If it isn't part of yours, why not?

In life and art we are constantly inspired by the world and people around us. So get yourself out of the house, out of your normal routine and let the world inspire you. Be sure to share with others, inspiring them if you can and you will be all the better for it.

Go forward in life and art, being thankful, giving credit where it is due and above all being inspired.

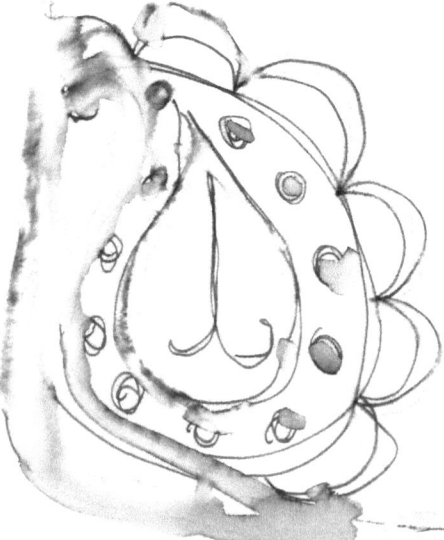

Where can you go or what can you do to shine your inspiring light on others and in return let them inspire you?

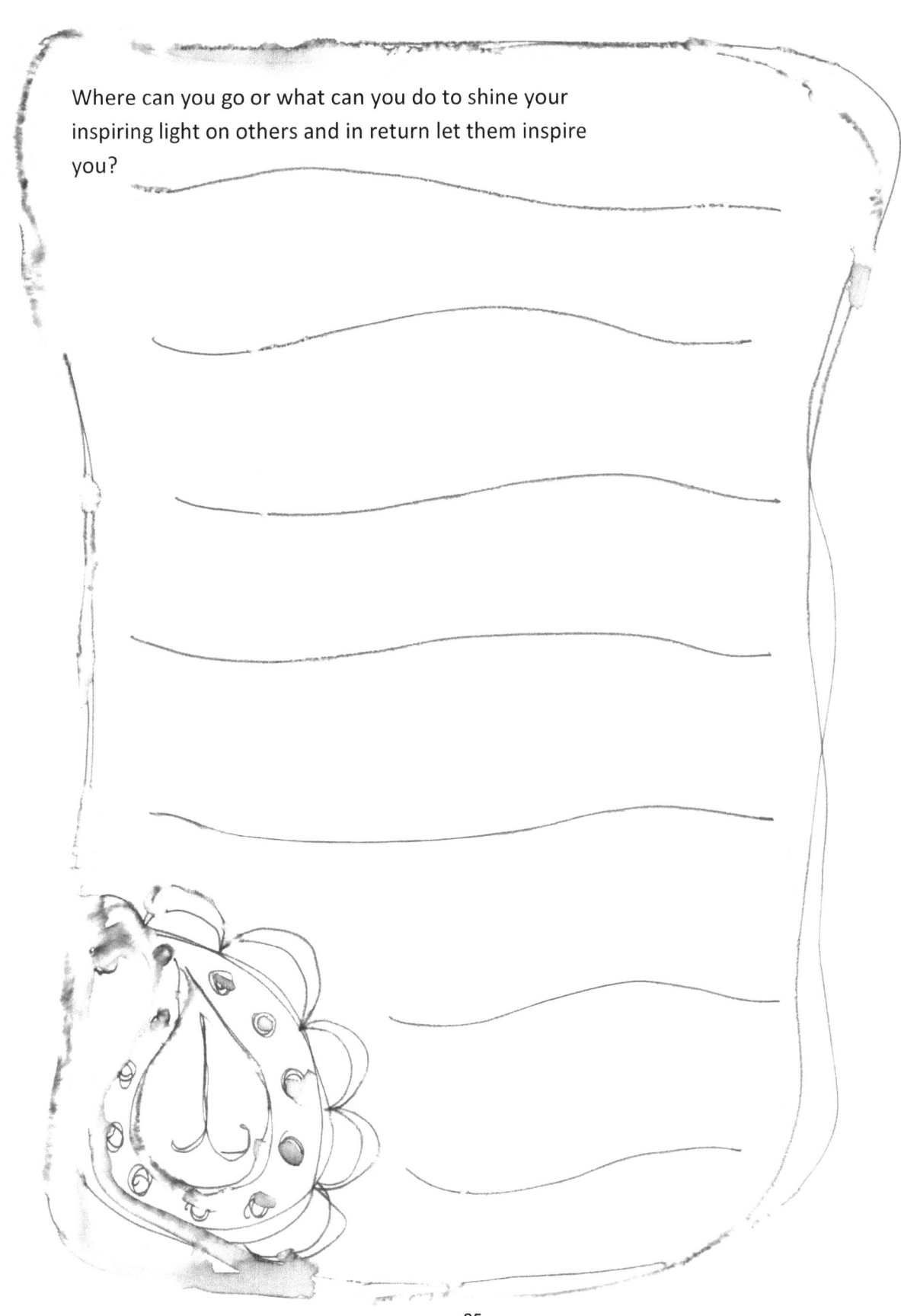

I tend to get single minded about things. I get an idea or project in my head and cannot do anything else until that is done. Even sometimes if it means I have sidetracked other things. No matter what I do I have always been, and still am, like this. I don't know if it's good or bad, it just is. I accept it and move on. Does it mean I have to cram sometimes to meet deadlines? Yes. I, however, do whatever is necessary to meet all deadlines. I accept, hug and welcome this part of me. It makes me who I am. It isn't going to change and I have better things to do than try.

Instead of fighting with who you are and where you are going, try being more accepting of yourself. Acknowledge who you are and where your journey is leading. Allow your path to be clear of this negativity so that your muse and inspirations can be let in.

Trying to be other than your true self is a waste of your time and everyone else's. So give yourself a hug. Welcome all those crazy, creaky, goofy parts and move on. You have better things to do, places to go and adventures to have.

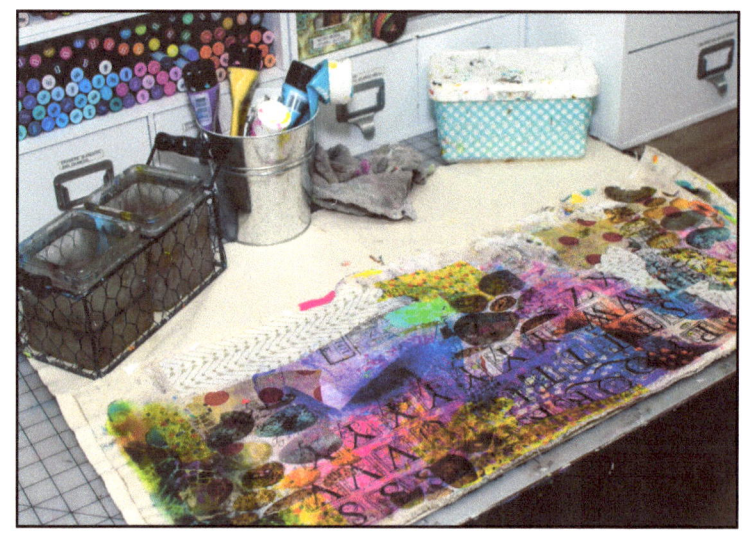

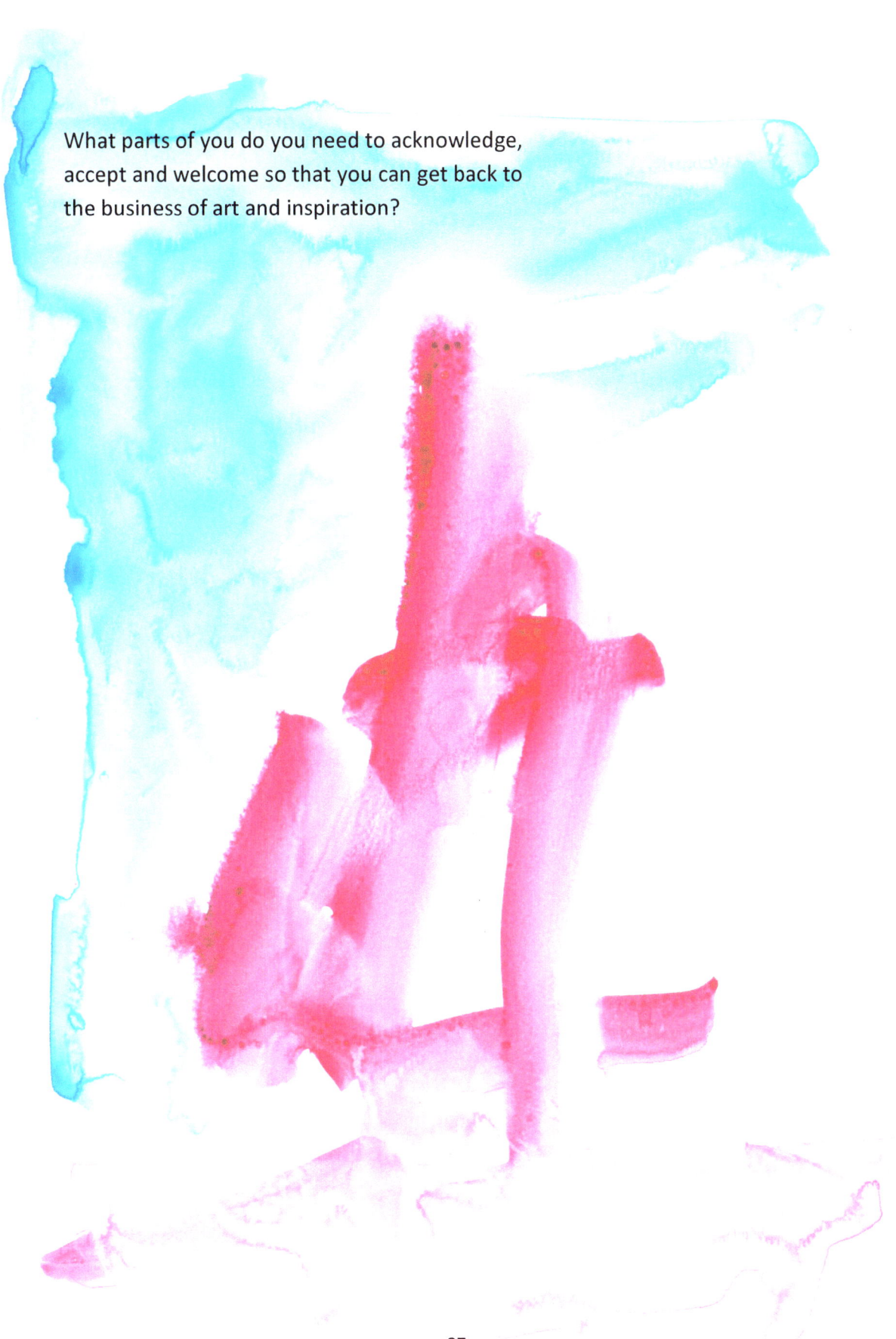

What parts of you do you need to acknowledge, accept and welcome so that you can get back to the business of art and inspiration?

Every now and then push yourself to do something you didn't think you could do. Try a new thing or go to a new place. Stretch yourself in new directions. Maybe even try something you don't think you are going to like. What is the worst that can happen? You find you really don't like it? Lesson learned.

Yielding to an unexpected surge of energy that I get when purging another closet or helping a fellow creative, helps me lighten and energize my soul. Gives fuel to my creative light. Life shouldn't always be about you. Open your eyes, look around and see who you can help today. You will find by helping others you are also finding new inspiration. Your soul will feel light enough to take flight and the ideas will start pouring in.

So the next time you are stuck maybe go volunteer at the library or school. Even doing things like sorting food at the food bank or donating blood can be inspiring. Maybe take a class on ceramics when the idea of it makes you twitch with anxiety over the mess. You will be amazed at what blossoms from just giving your soul a chance to stretch and grow.

What can you do that is new, unexpected and maybe something you don't think you will enjoy? What joy can you spread to others that will in turn lighten and brighten your soul? Give your muse a little push or maybe a kick in the arse and see where it leads you. You may fall down from the kick, but you may land in a bead of roses.

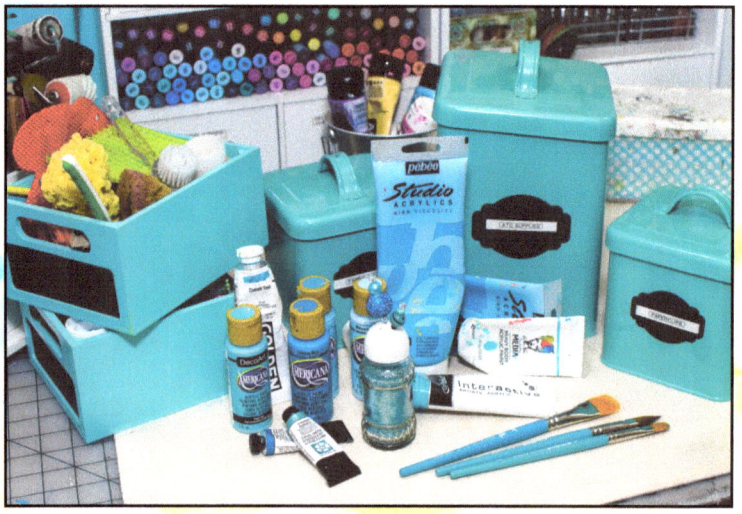

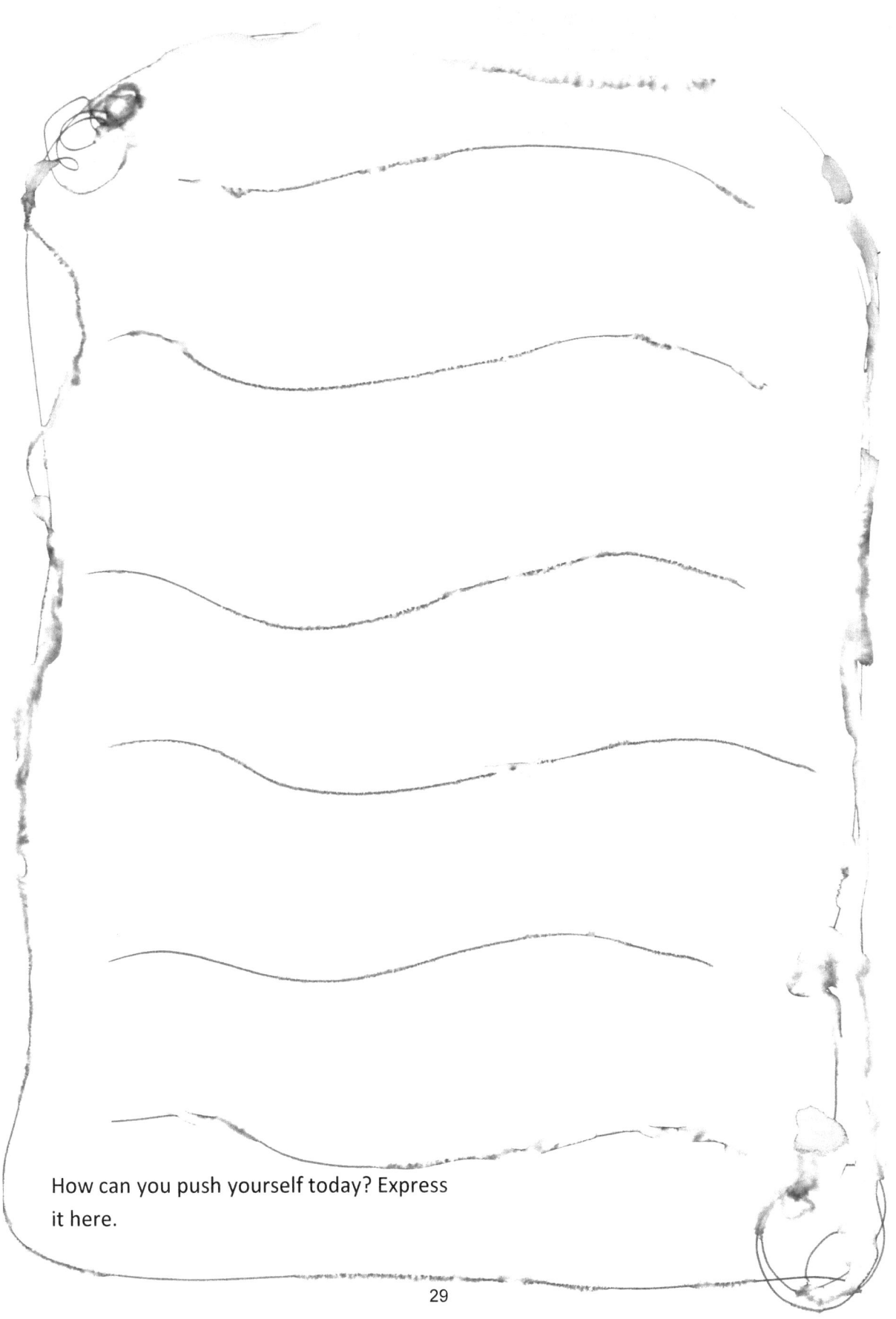

How can you push yourself today? Express
it here.

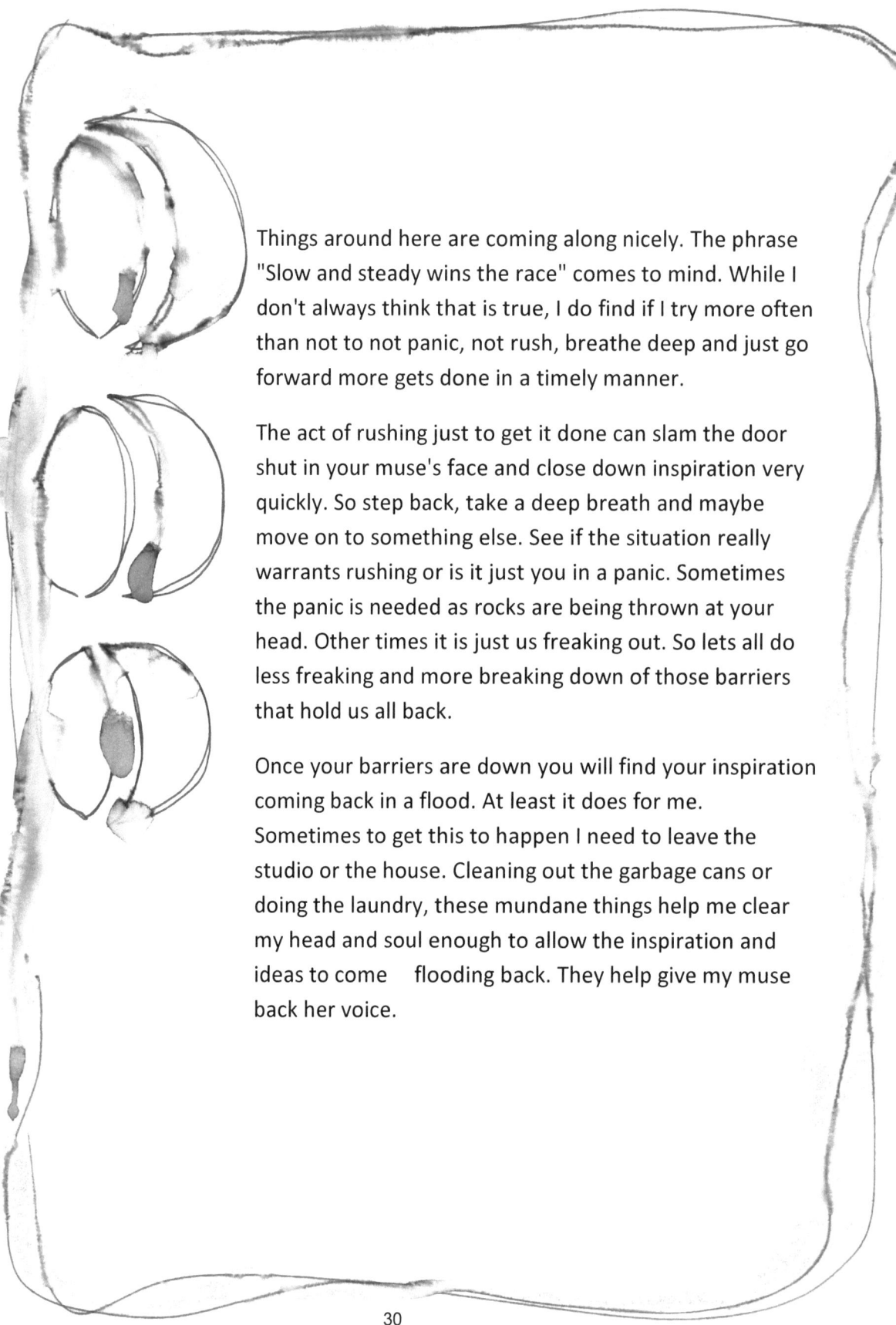

Things around here are coming along nicely. The phrase "Slow and steady wins the race" comes to mind. While I don't always think that is true, I do find if I try more often than not to not panic, not rush, breathe deep and just go forward more gets done in a timely manner.

The act of rushing just to get it done can slam the door shut in your muse's face and close down inspiration very quickly. So step back, take a deep breath and maybe move on to something else. See if the situation really warrants rushing or is it just you in a panic. Sometimes the panic is needed as rocks are being thrown at your head. Other times it is just us freaking out. So lets all do less freaking and more breaking down of those barriers that hold us all back.

Once your barriers are down you will find your inspiration coming back in a flood. At least it does for me. Sometimes to get this to happen I need to leave the studio or the house. Cleaning out the garbage cans or doing the laundry, these mundane things help me clear my head and soul enough to allow the inspiration and ideas to come   flooding back. They help give my muse back her voice.

What can you do when you are tempted to rush or panic?

get real
with
yourself →

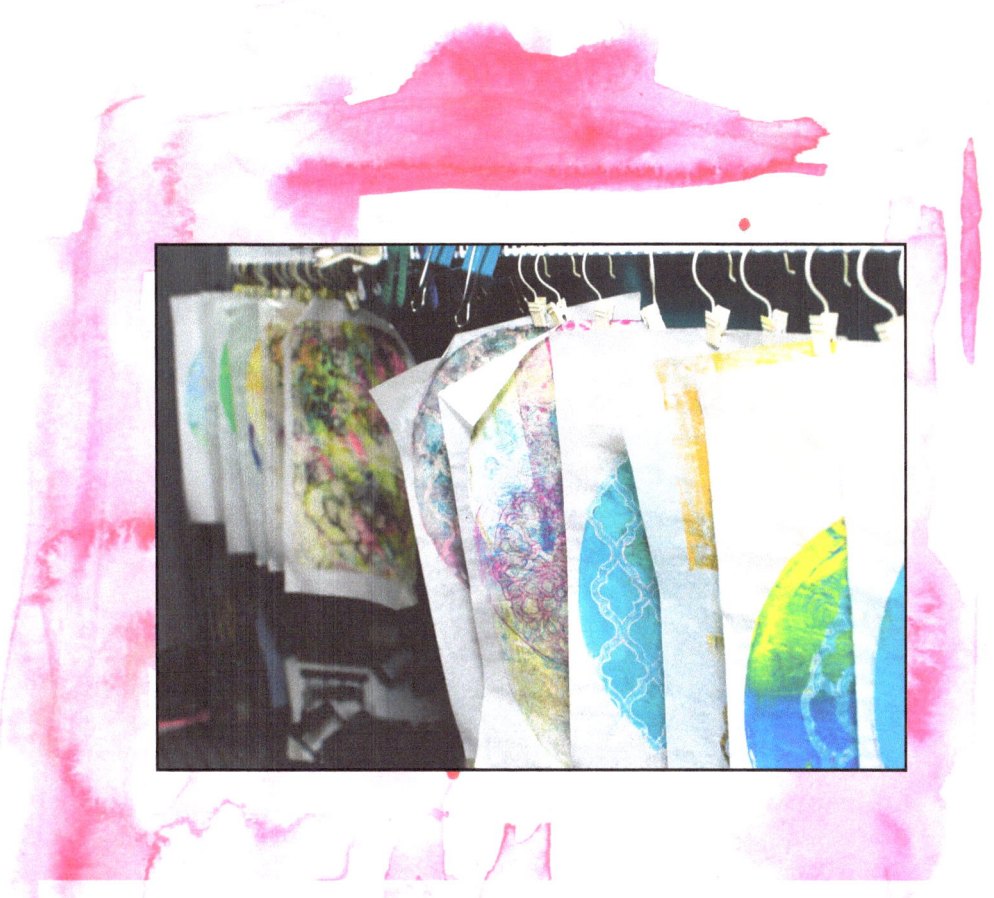

Acknowledging Your Feelings:

"If I can step out of my comfort zone, grow, learn and experience more of this creative life, then so can you. Life is short. It is time to pull up those big girl panties and take a deep breath. Just step forward. Life is too short to let fears hold you back from doing what you love, expressing who you are and being who you were meant to be. Embrace your feelings. Accept and enjoy them. Remember that your journey is your journey and that the route you take doesn't matter as long as it makes you happy. "

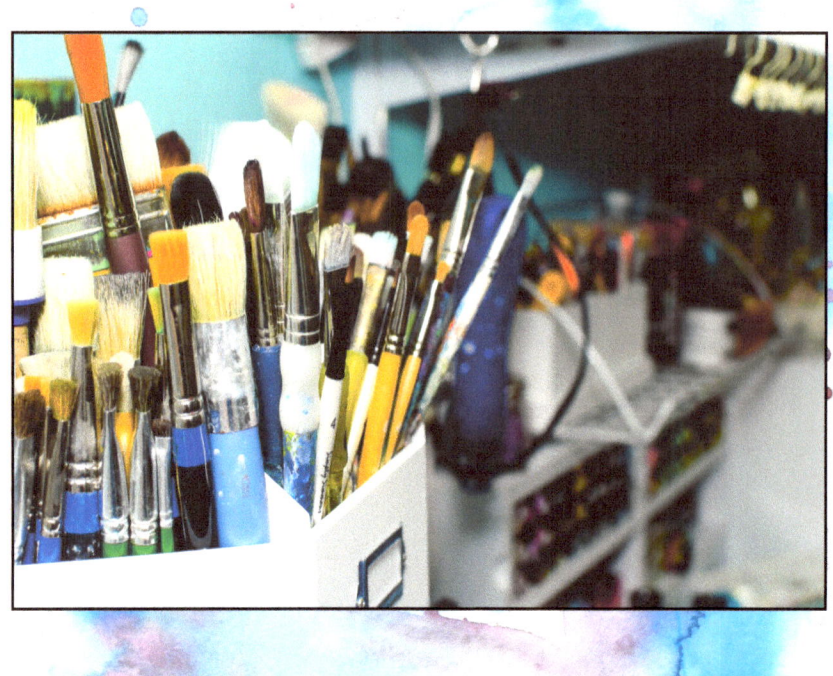

My therapist once told me that people who like to be in control, and don't deal well with things not being in control, are those most likely to have anxiety disorder. Wow did she have me pegged with that statement.

Worrying about, and stressing about, what other people think of you and your work is so not worth it. Stressing over that which we cannot control is a huge waste of time. Yes, if you are trying to sell your work you care a bit if others like it, but ultimately you must first find joy in what you are doing. I firmly believe it will show in your work which others will notice.

People may joke and chuckle about you trying a new path, but ignore them. You can't control what they think, so don't even try. Do what is right for you. Those that truly love you will support and even encourage you.

Other people cannot make you happy, only you can make you happy. Do something this weekend that sets you on the right path to this end. I dare you!

What can you do to let go of the stress of what you can't control?
How can you be better about accepting yourself for who you are
and not caring what others think?

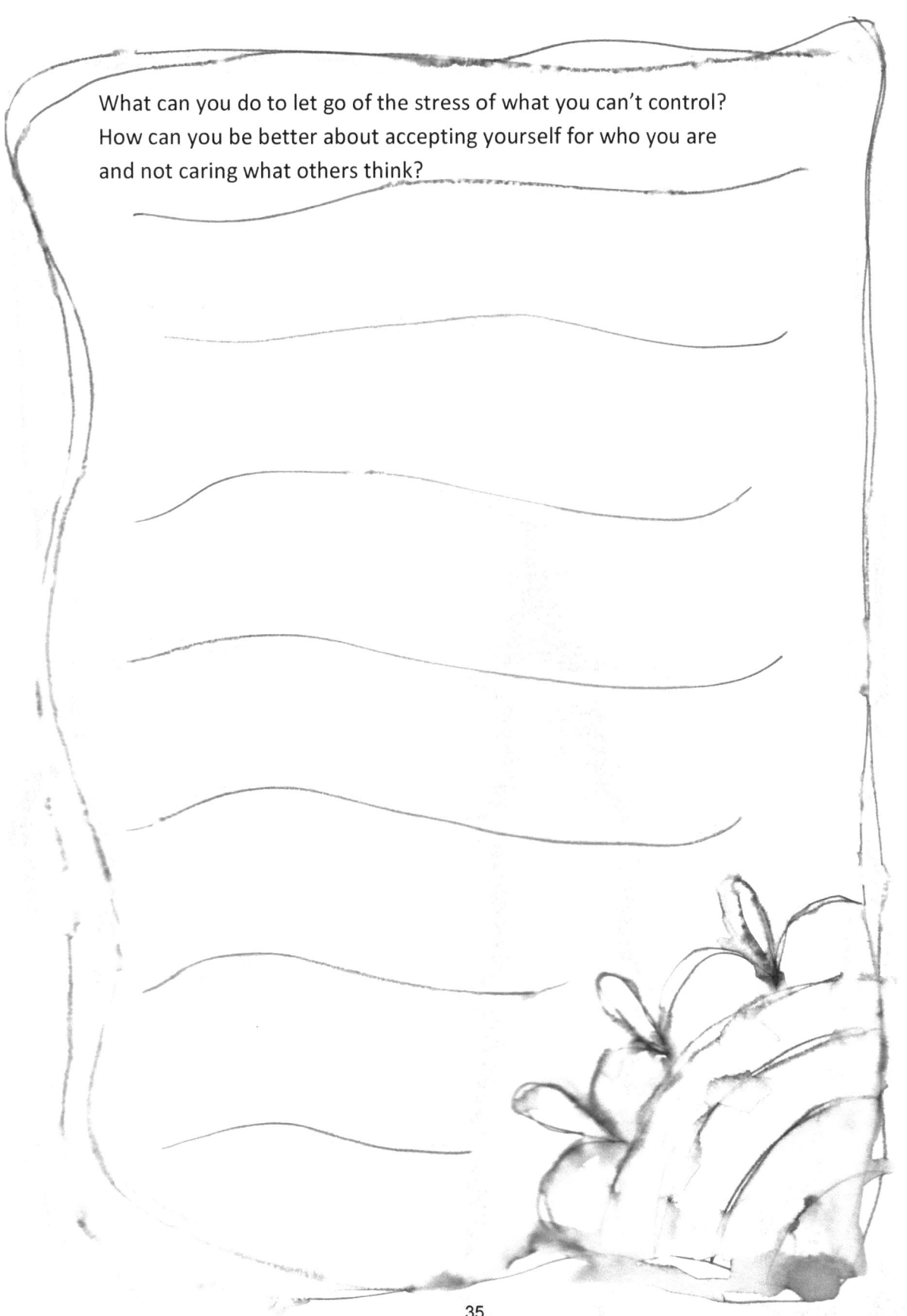

It shouldn't take a great effort to be kind to each other or to be encouraging. I just don't understand not being that way. Don't people have better things to do than cause others mental harm and angst? I know I do.

I would rather create art and pretty things and to encourage others to do the same. I would like to inspire you all to be all you can and all you want to be. I am sending good positive energy out to you all.

That is where I want my time and energy to go. How about you guys? Helping others with kind words rather than negative helps everyone. What's that old saying? "You can catch more flies with honey than vinegar." I am not sure it is true, but it couldn't hurt to try.

My way of paying it forward is to encourage all of you to be who you want to and were meant to be. There is no wrong way, only your way. There is no judgment or negativity, only encouragement and   support.

I am not someone who likes to waste time being negative. I don't want that energy in my life or my art. It does happen sometimes. I am only human but I try not to dwell on it too much. I do my best to move forward and not look back. I like to promote good, positive and encouraging feelings, not negative ones.

What have you done recently to encourage your fellow creatives? How can you help to help lift them up and not break them down? What have you done to help yourself? Do you get the same energetic boost I do from helping others? Don't know? Try it and see. You may help them but also yourself in the process.

Try changing your way of thinking and do something to encourage

another.....I dare you.

What steps can you take to cut some of the negativity from your life and your art? How can you be more encouraging of your fellow creatives? How does it make you feel?

OK, so this morning I am stalling because I have a chore I don't really want to do. I am being kind to myself and working my way into it. I have to go through all my craft show merchandise and fixtures. I need to decide what will sell online and what won't. I then need to donate what won't to charity or other artists. I have dreaded this chore for a long while and cannot begin to tell you how much I am not looking forward to it.

I am not going to beat myself up because I don't handle certain things well. I will probably not be doing too many shows in the future. I am going to accept this part of me and give her a hug. Let her know it is going to be ok and this is part of moving forward.

No, moving forward isn't always easy. Sometimes it is really hard and painful. Staying stuck in a rut because I don't want to deal with difficult things does not serve me well. It won't serve you well either.

How can you help yourself to move forward? What changes or help do you need to make that happen? Whatever changes you may be going thru right now, no matter how big or small, know that it is ok! There is no shame in seeking help if you need it. Give yourself a hug and move forward, even if it is only in baby steps.

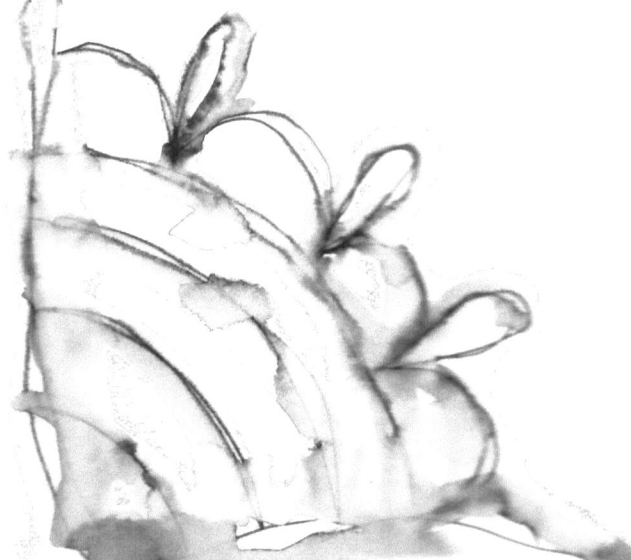

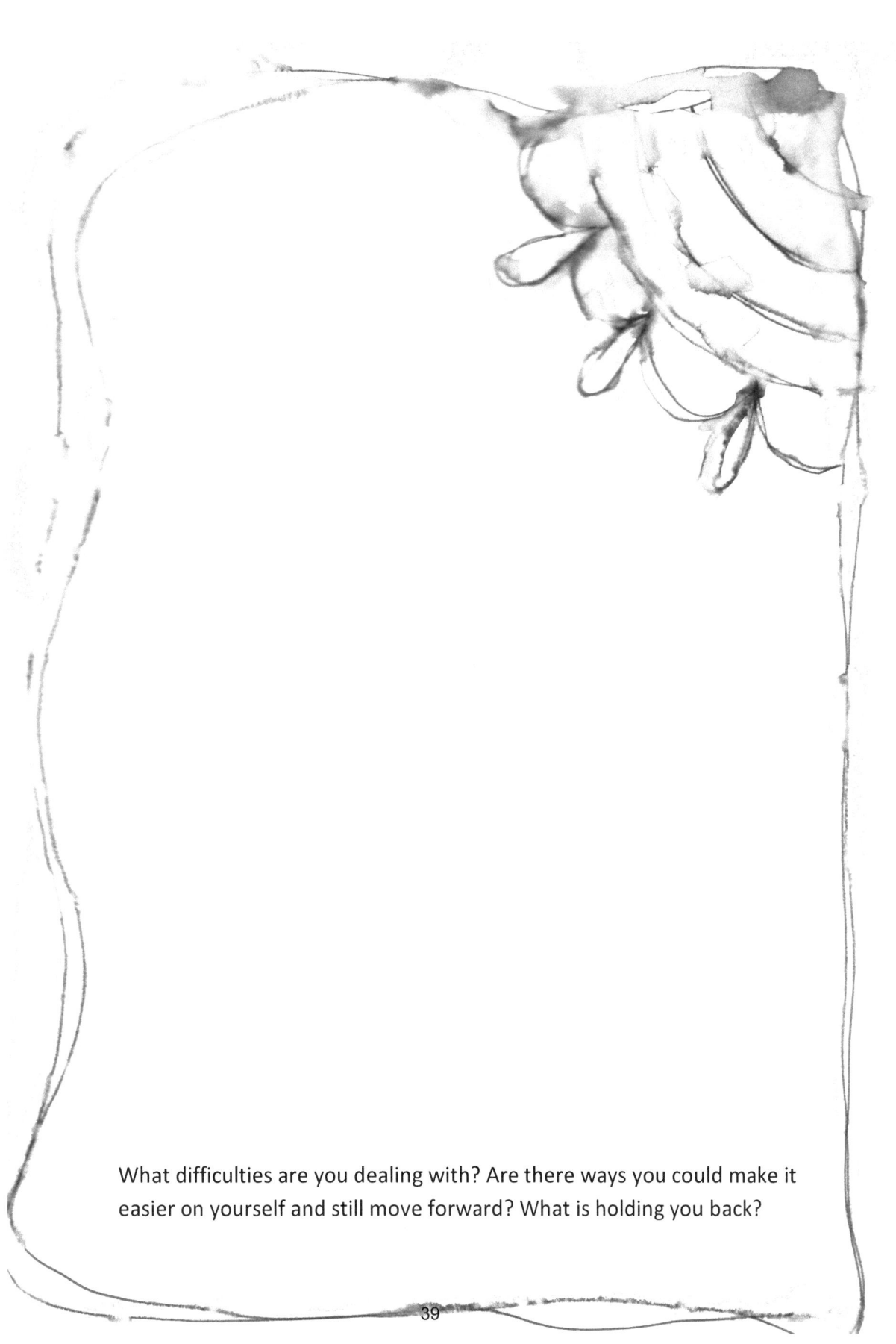

What difficulties are you dealing with? Are there ways you could make it easier on yourself and still move forward? What is holding you back?

I use to tell people that I was a paranoid, impatient, pessimist, who likes to be in control, but I am working on it. That wasn't exactly true. I am a paranoid, anxiety driven, impatient, depressive, pessimist, who likes to be in control. I embrace that and own it. I am not really working to change it, rather learning to live with it and not drive everyone I love around me away. I have things that help me cope like my sticky notes, lists and art. I am learning that music and exercise also help. For now, I have chosen to not take any more medications.

I am not telling you this to brag or get attention. This is just so that you know you are not alone. We all have issues. Embrace your faults as well as your attributes. They make you the unique person you are.

Art, among other things, is great therapy. It can help you work through issues you may be dealing with. Try it! Don't be afraid to seek professional help if you need it. Even on a budget there are usually options.

What other things do you do to help get through the rough patches? What could you do differently?

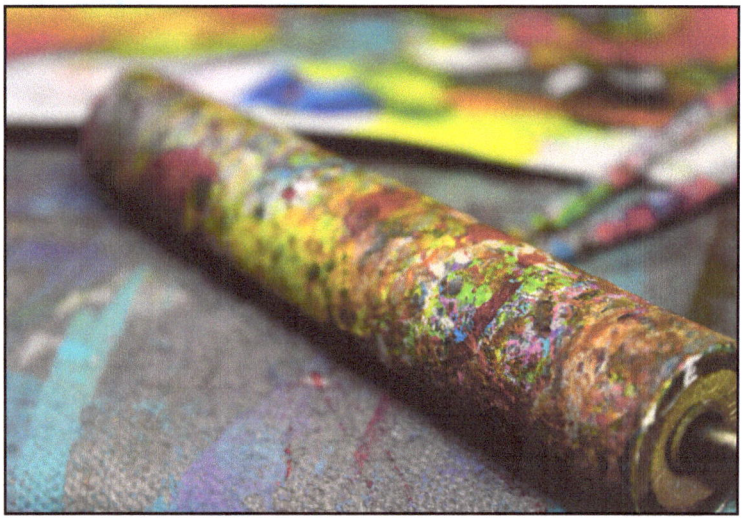

Have you accepted who you are? Do you have ways of dealing with the rough stuff? What is working? What isn't?

Ever have a moment where you think, "If I say what I truly think or feel they will either slap me, hate me or both?" Both of my Grandmothers always said "If you don't have anything nice to say, don't say anything at all." I am sure your Grandmothers said it also. When speaking to a fellow creative soul, tempering your words with kindness is even more important. I am not advocating lying. Not ever! But truths can be told kindly instead of harshly.

Art is great therapy for working out those things that bother you. So when stressed, break out your creativity and start working. Instead of being harsh to those around you, or yourself, work through the stress in your art. Get it out of your soul and onto the page. Before you know it things will be fine. Just don't forget to breathe.

The next time you are tempted to harshness, remember temperance. When speaking to a fellow creative, or more importantly yourself, speak with kindness in your heart and love in your soul. Tempering the written or spoken word with kindness costs nothing but means the world to those hearing it, especially yourself.

How can you be kinder to yourself? To others? How can you release the stress in a healthier way without exploding all over those around you?

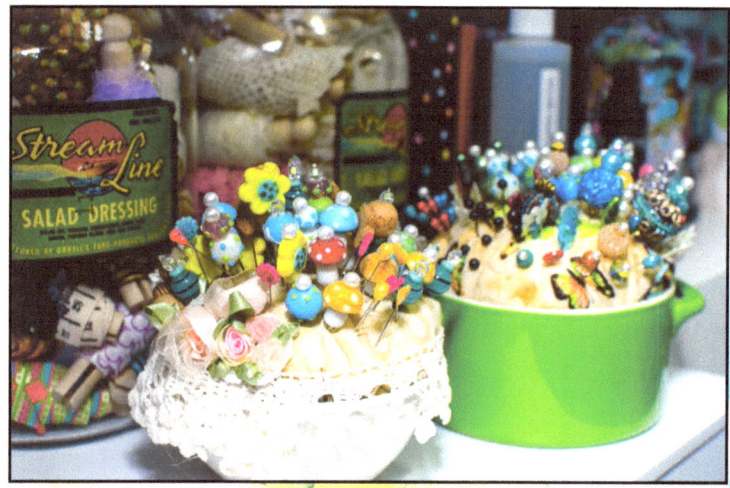

What can you do differently to be
kinder to yourself and others?

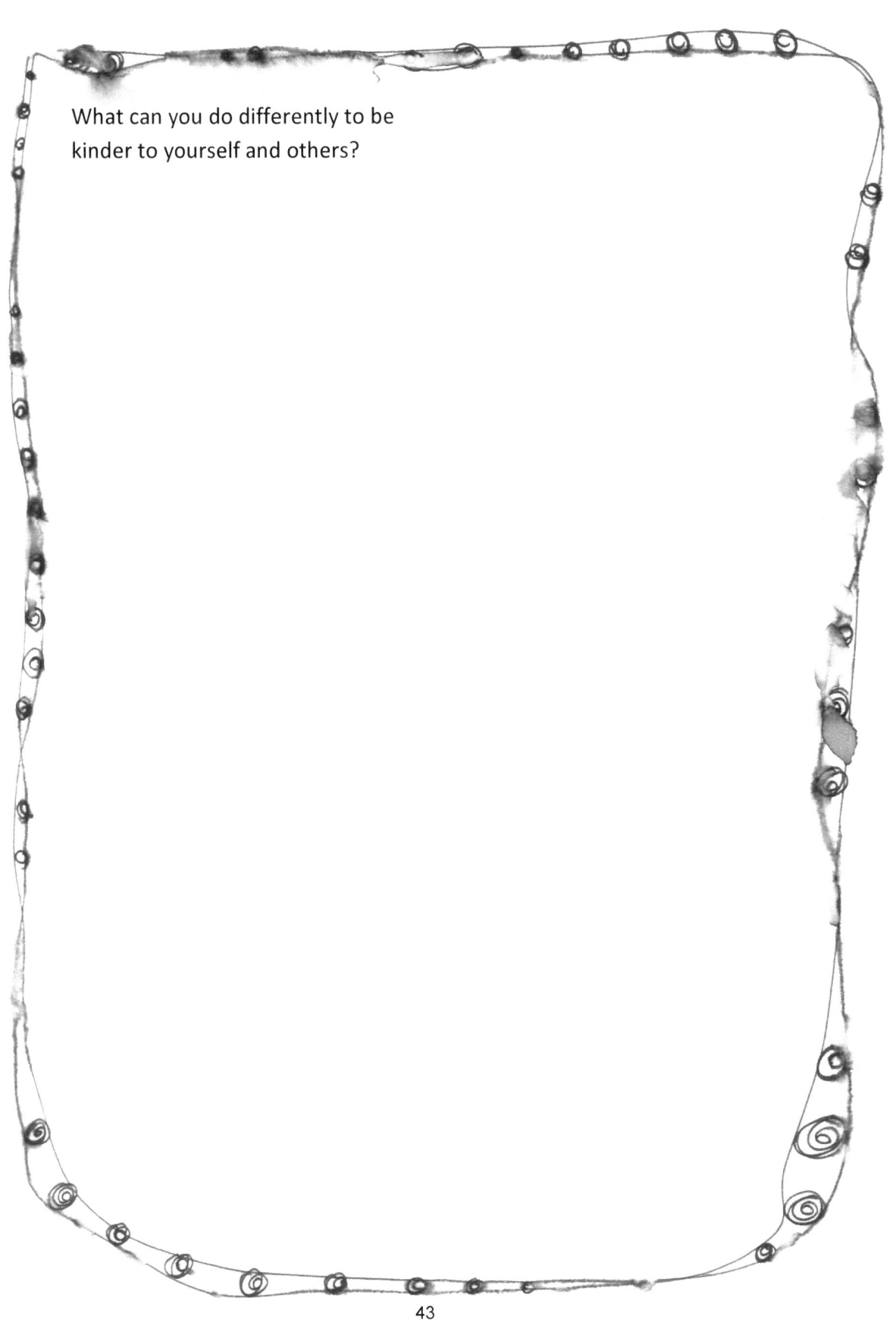

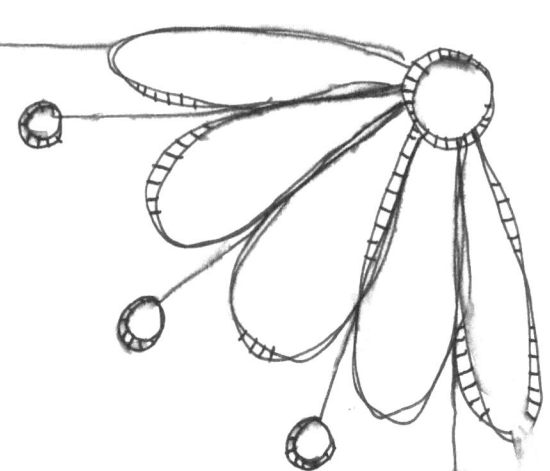

We all have our off days. Those days when it feels like life woke up and gave you a big ol' smack in the face. I have said many times in my life that I know the supreme being is testing me and he knows I can handle it. Sometimes I need a break and wish he would go test someone else right now.

Have you ever felt like that? Know that when this happens, and it will, that you are not alone. We all have these moments in life. It is how we handle them that makes the difference. Let go of what we cannot change and learn to change or react differently to those things that we can.

A successful life is not about money, it is about a lot of hard work. There is no short cut. Believe me, I would let you know if there was. Being happy is hard work. Crawling into a hole and pulling up the covers is easy, but wont make you happy. Express yourself, dark or light, into your art. Let it go and release it so that you can get on with your life and enjoy it.

Our time on this earth is finite. As my dad would say, "Enjoy it while you are still on the right side of the dirt."

Can you express how you are feeling right now? Can you accept and release it? Can you accept it is OK to be happy?

"Don't lose site of who you are in life. Stay the path to create the life you want in creativity, light and love."

Gina B Ahrens

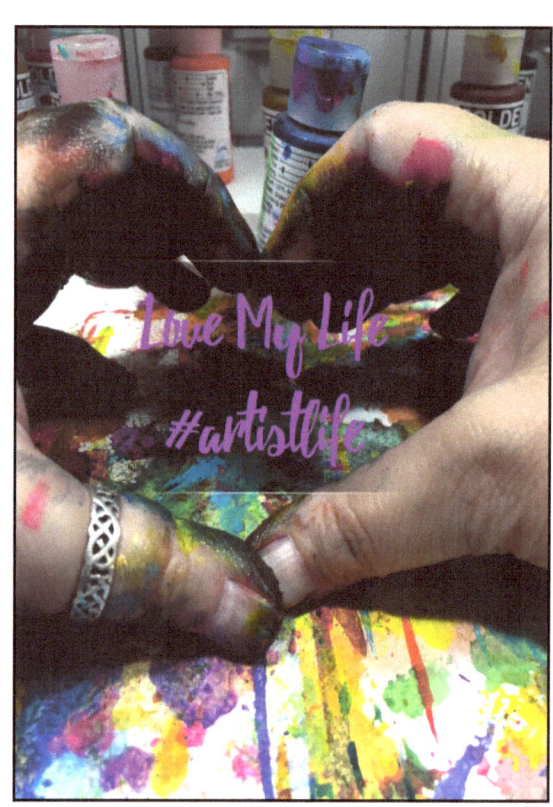

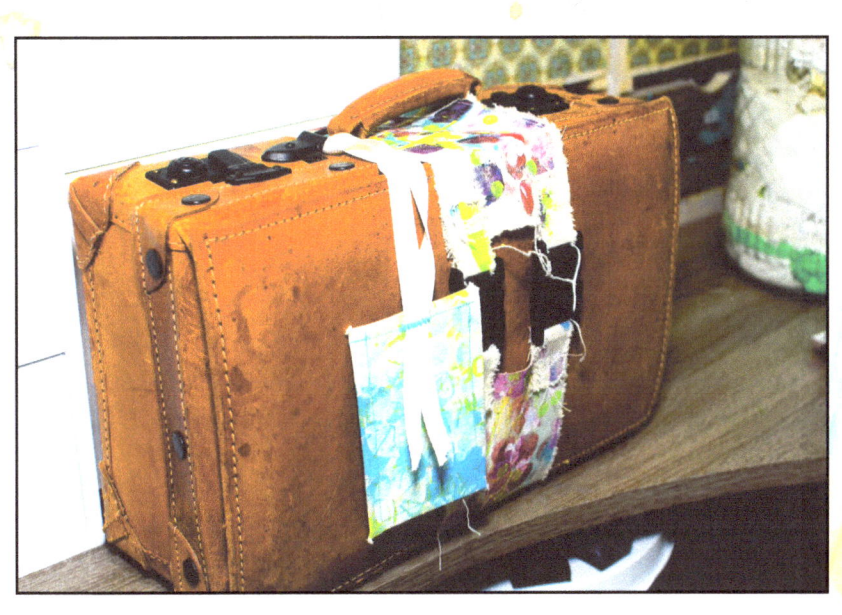

Your Life's Path:

"Life is a journey that should be enjoyed. To continue to be creative we must move forward. Creativity feeds the soul but must be nurtured. A creative life is not always easy. It can be challenging and stressful. The rewards, though, can be enormous. To continue we must move forward in the bright light of our own fabulous journey. So take the ride of your life on it's forward path and enjoy the view. You won't regret it and anyway what have you got to lose?"

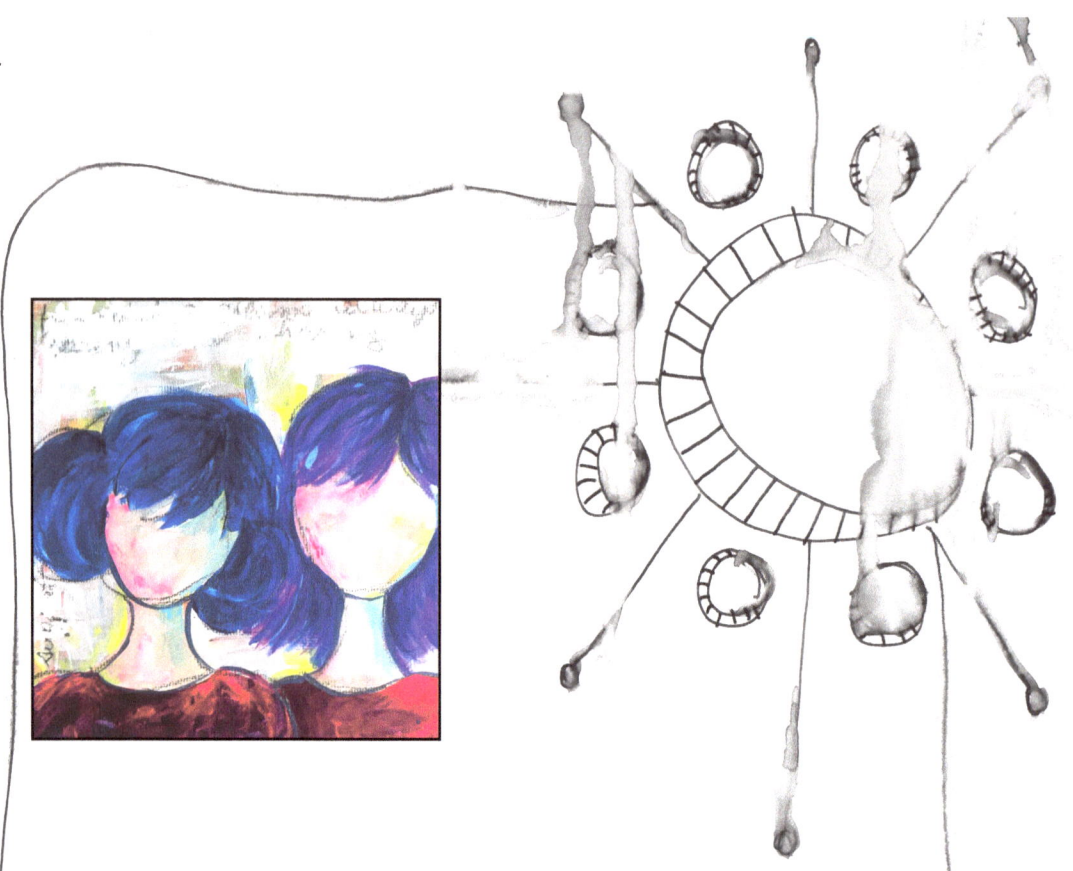

Choosing to live a creative, respectful and expressive life does not always go over well with others, but this is my path and my choice. Those I love understand. Those that don't, well to be honest, saddens me, but does not concern me.

Making this choice is not an easy one. You will run into many obstacles. Do not be detoured. Stay the path and do what you need to in order to be happy, while also being respectful of those around you.

Sometimes you need to step away and take a break in order to find your true path again and that is ok. Don't beat yourself up about it. It is also part of your creative process.

Have you ever had moments like this? What can you do, or do you need to do, differently to achieve this?

Know you are not alone.

Have you made your choices? Do You Know your
path? What do you need to do to get there?

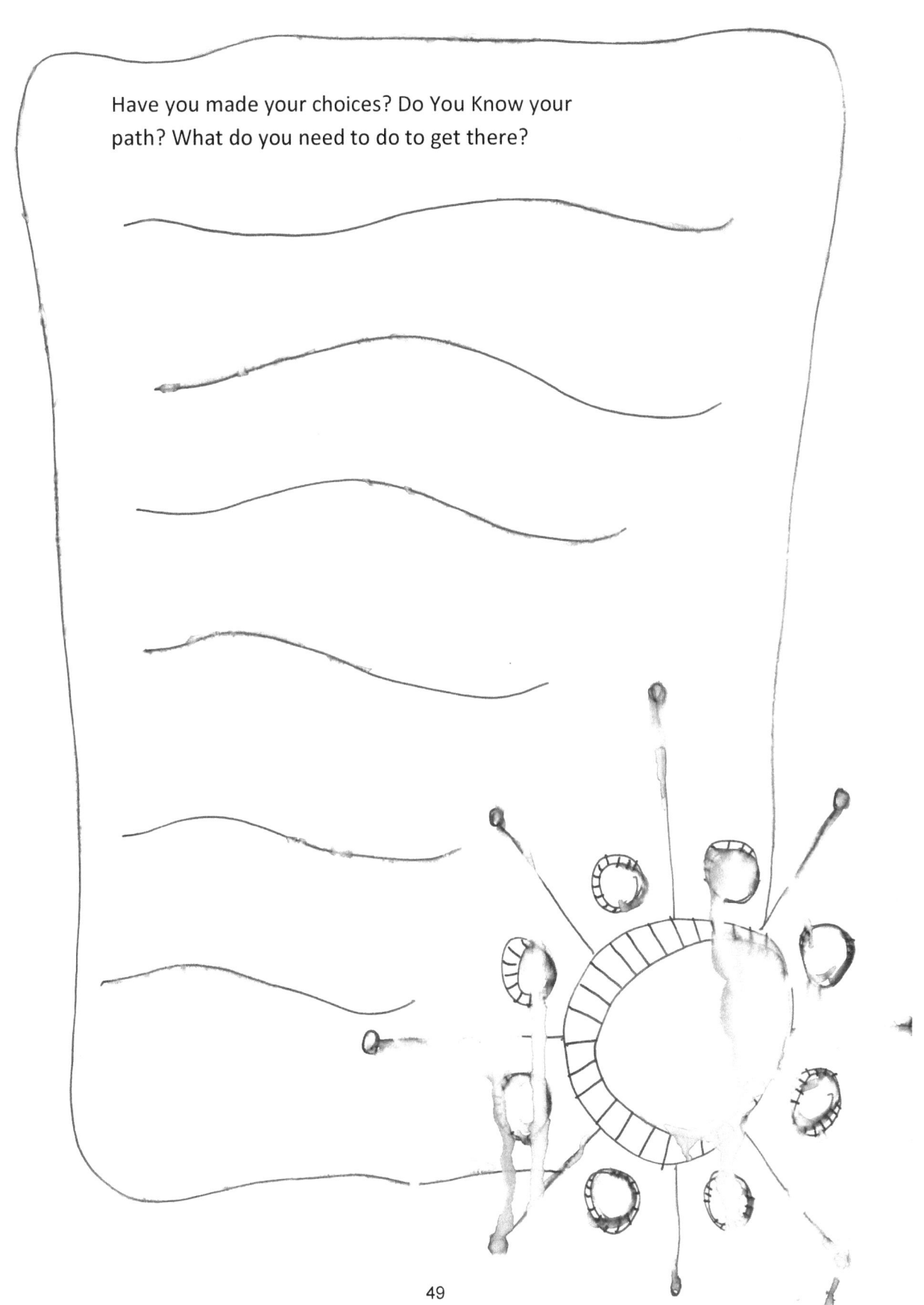

Do you see the glass half empty or half full? Do you see the possibilities in the glass and it's beauty?

My first instinct is to see it half empty and overlook the beauty of the glass. As I have grown older, grown in art and life, I try to ignore that first instinct. But, yes, it is still there. I work on seeing the beauty of the glass no matter how much may be in it. This is something we should all strive for.

I am by nature a shy introvert. In school I only graduated because my teacher took pity on me and gave me a D in speech because I just couldn't do it no matter how hard I tried. I did try and made a terrible fool of myself. That was a long time ago, but I learned from that to just take a deep breath, step forward and try. If I fail it isn't because I didn't try. You will never succeed unless you take that first step.

I dare you to look at the beauty of the glass, to try what terrifies you. Even if you fail it will be a learning and growing experience that will set you down that much farther on your life's path toward your goals. Don't let those obstacles or potholes stop you from where you really want to go. Try a new path that will get you to that same destination.

If the worst part of your day is having to get a magnifying mirror and your reading glasses to use the tweezers, then go outside for really good lighting in order to find all those pesky menopausal mustache hairs then your day is going pretty good. Yes I know you men are cringing or laughing or both. Sorry. If I can find those damned mustache hairs that I can barely see then you can do this too. I know you can.

Life frequently doesn't go as planned. We need to learn to roll with the punches, distractions and detours. Learn to stay standing in the hurricane force winds, to be brave and create!

What have you been scared or hesitant to try and do? What is holding you back? Try looking at things a new way or from a new perspective. Like seeing the beauty of the glass instead of its contents. Try something new......I dare you.

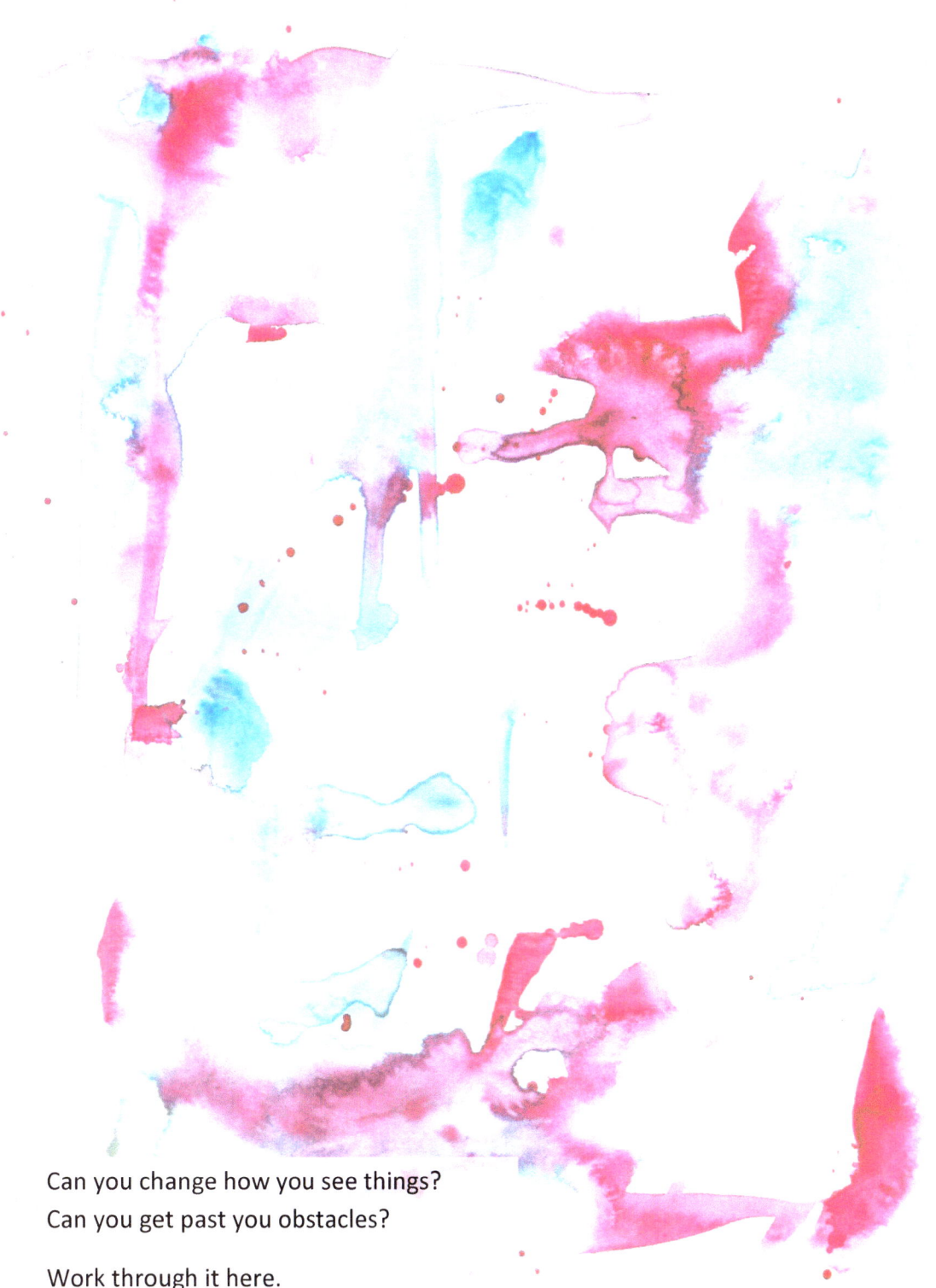

Can you change how you see things?
Can you get past you obstacles?

Work through it here.

What do you have that you need to let go of? That causes you stress? Remember that your life will not end if you don't get it done. It isn't the end of the world, and yes, I know sometimes this is easier said than done. Lol.

Some days I sit at my desk and wonder where to get started. Maybe I forgot to make a list the night before or maybe the list is very long. Either way when I feel overwhelmed. I just don't know where to get started. I know you all feel this way sometimes, too.

I usually start working through this by re-prioritizing my list, by deciding what has to be done today and what can wait. Just because I think certain things needed to get done yesterday doesn't mean they really needed to. Those who know me know I am not the most patient of souls on a good day and that is being kind to myself.

I try to take a deep breath and just stop. I know it sounds silly but it helps ground and redirect me. Then I can find what truly needs doing and get it done. Filming for instance happens all the time....but editing needs only doing once a week or so.

So remember today to stop and take a deep breath. Climb down from the cliffs edge that anxiety has you perched on. Do the things that cannot be put off and the rest can wait.

How can you better handle your life's stresses?
What do you need to let go of?

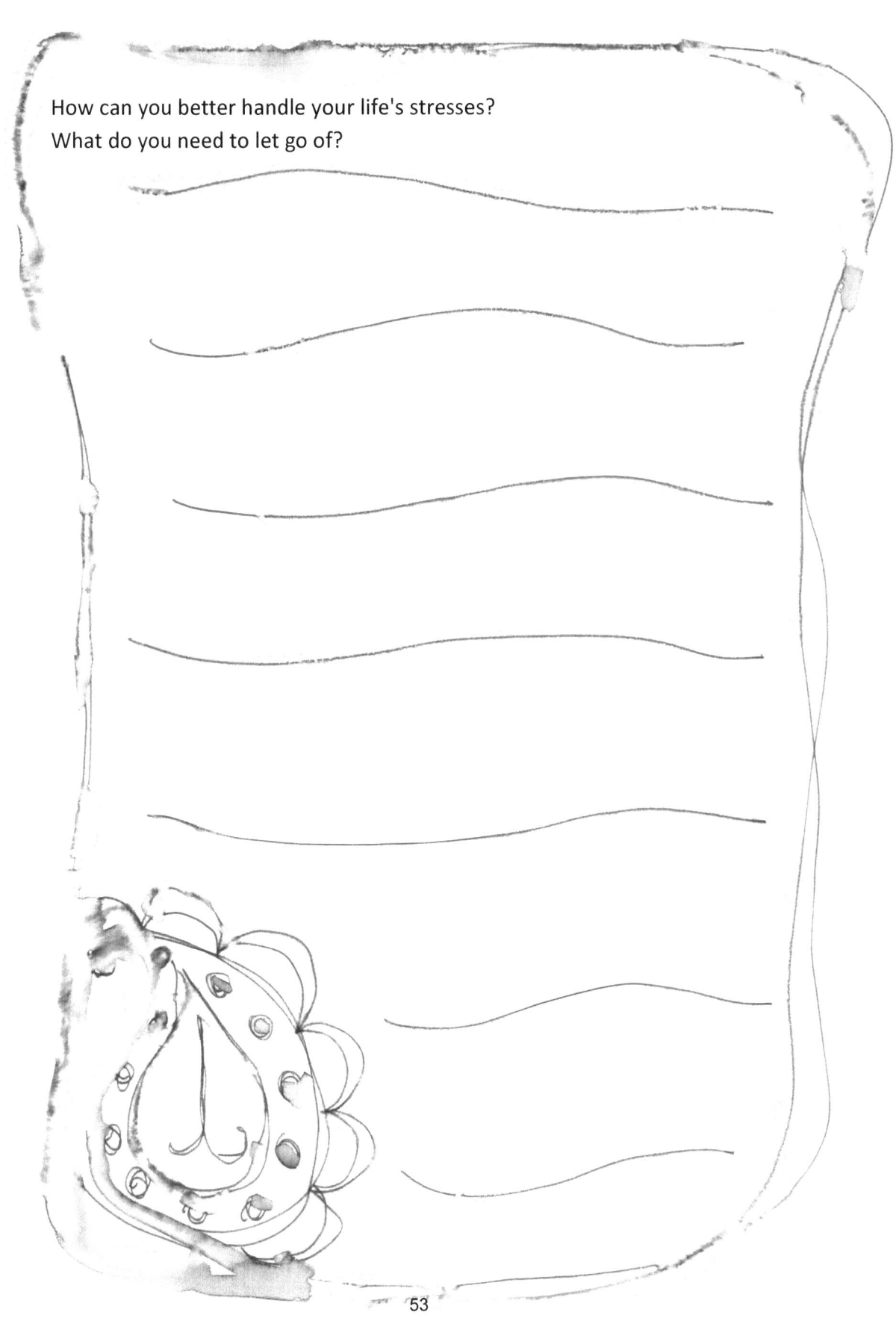

When reflecting today on my life's path and how much it has changed from where I thought it would go, I never in a million years, thought I would spend the second half of my life immersed in art, helping others express themselves creatively or, of all things, on YouTube.

I had no idea there would be such a thing as the internet and as a shy kid with severe stage fright there was no way was I going be on camera. Ever! Boy howdy how things have changed.

You never know where life's path will take you. I believe there is a pre-destined plan for all of us. Something we are suppose to learn or experience on our path. Good or bad my path has lead me to where I am today and I rejoice in that.

Find that thing for you that makes you whole, allows your spirit to sing and fly. Listen to your own inner voice and follow that path in life to peace. Your spirit knows the way....you just need to listen.

Take a deep breath and find comfort in knowing your path has a destination. Your spirit knows the way.

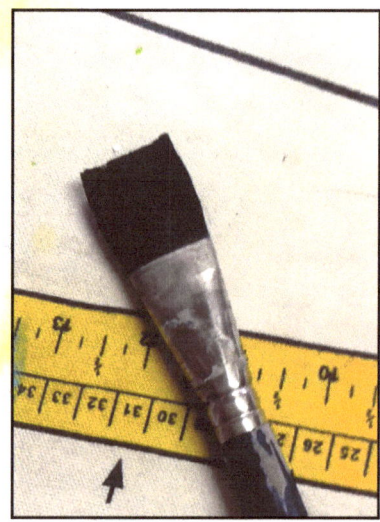

Where did you think you were going in life?
Where did you end up? Are you happy? Do
you need to make changes?

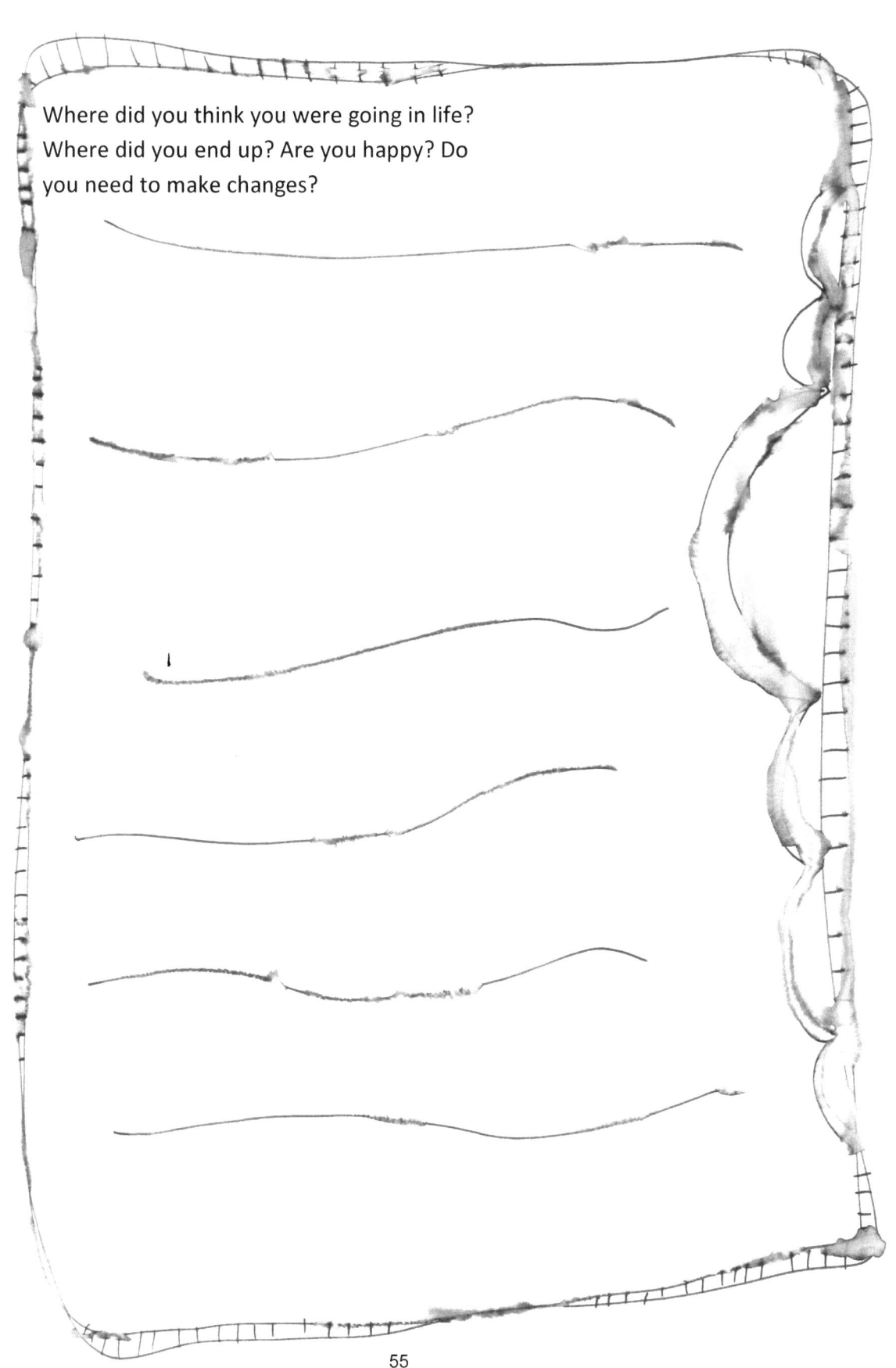

Have you ever done art in practice or a lesson that you are not really excited about? I have. Why? There is always something to be learned. Always! I mean, really, who wants to draw eyes a million times, but by the end you would be damn good at it. Whether it is a lesson I am taking or a prompt I am suppose to teach, the projects I am not really feeling are the ones I always learn the most from.

Remember to count the little wins. Sometimes they are more important than the big ones. Practicing and learning, wins and losses are all part of our growth as a human being. The lessons learned from the negative are just as important as the positive. They all lead us down the path on our life's journey.

So remember those small steps, wins, learning lessons or triumphs that are taking you on the right path. They are super important. Let these experiences lead you down the path to where your soul is happiest. These steps may not seem like much at first, but trust me they are huge when you take a look back.

Life, like art, is a learning experience. I cherish all the moments....good bad or indifferent. It is part of my path and journey. So instead of discouragement from failures, try and glean what you have learned from them, because there is always something to be learned. There is time enough to stop learning and growing when we pass to the next place.

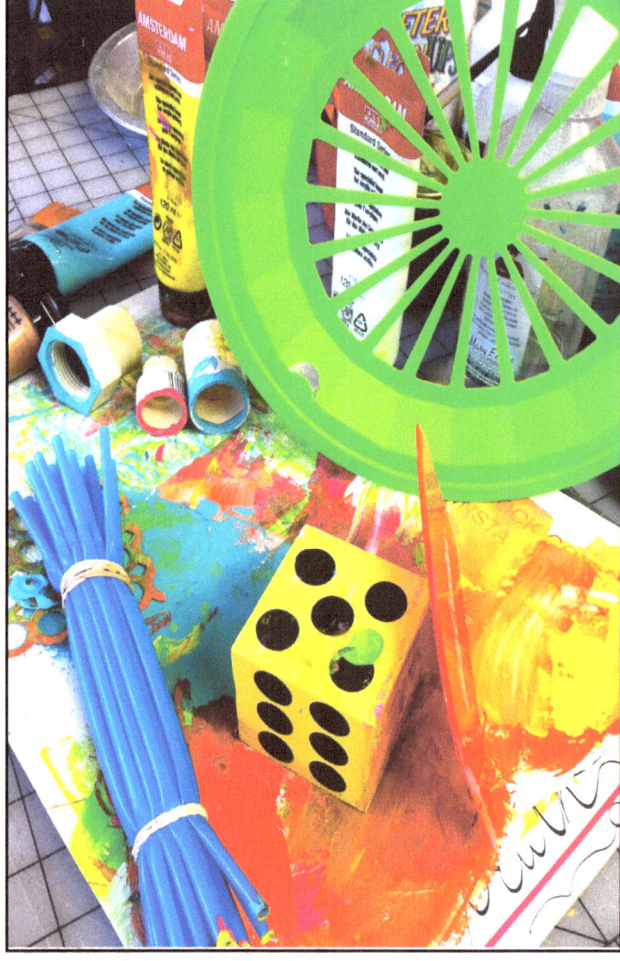

Can you celebrate your wins and losses? Have you learned what you need to from your experiences?

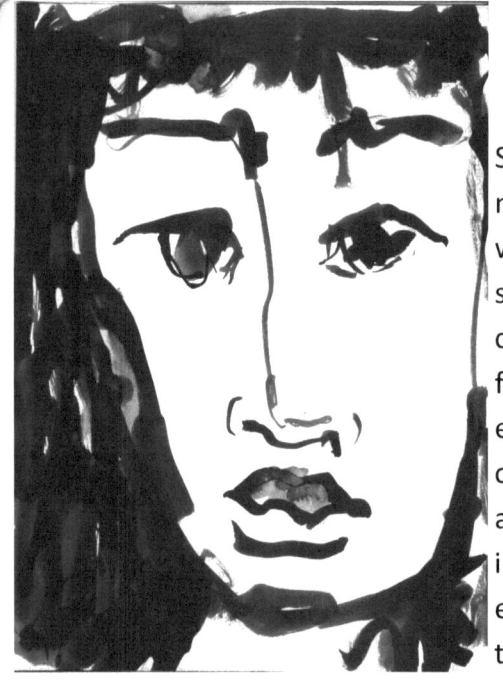

Sometimes in life, the choices we make have a huge effect on the world around us, other times not so much or at least it seems. The choices you make in life going forward, whether hard ones or easy, have a ripple effect not only on the rest of your life but those around you. Like a pebble thrown into the water, those ripples expand and effect other things in the pond.

Make your choices knowing this but also knowing true to your heart what is the right choice for you.

These choices are never easy and we are always aware of the results to the world around us, at least most of us are. Being true to yourself and what you need to do to be happy, opening yourself up to the possibility of happiness will allow those others in to share that bright light with you.

Sometimes life has other plans for us, our day or event than we would wish or expect. Let go and try to roll with the message the universe is trying to give you, even if it isn't one you really want to hear. Maybe you need to hear it anyway.

Whatever your dreams and goals are I know they can be accomplished. By taking baby steps, if needed, as long as they are in the right direction, you will get there.

Keep your eye on the prize as you journey down life's path. Be determined, be driven and you will get there.

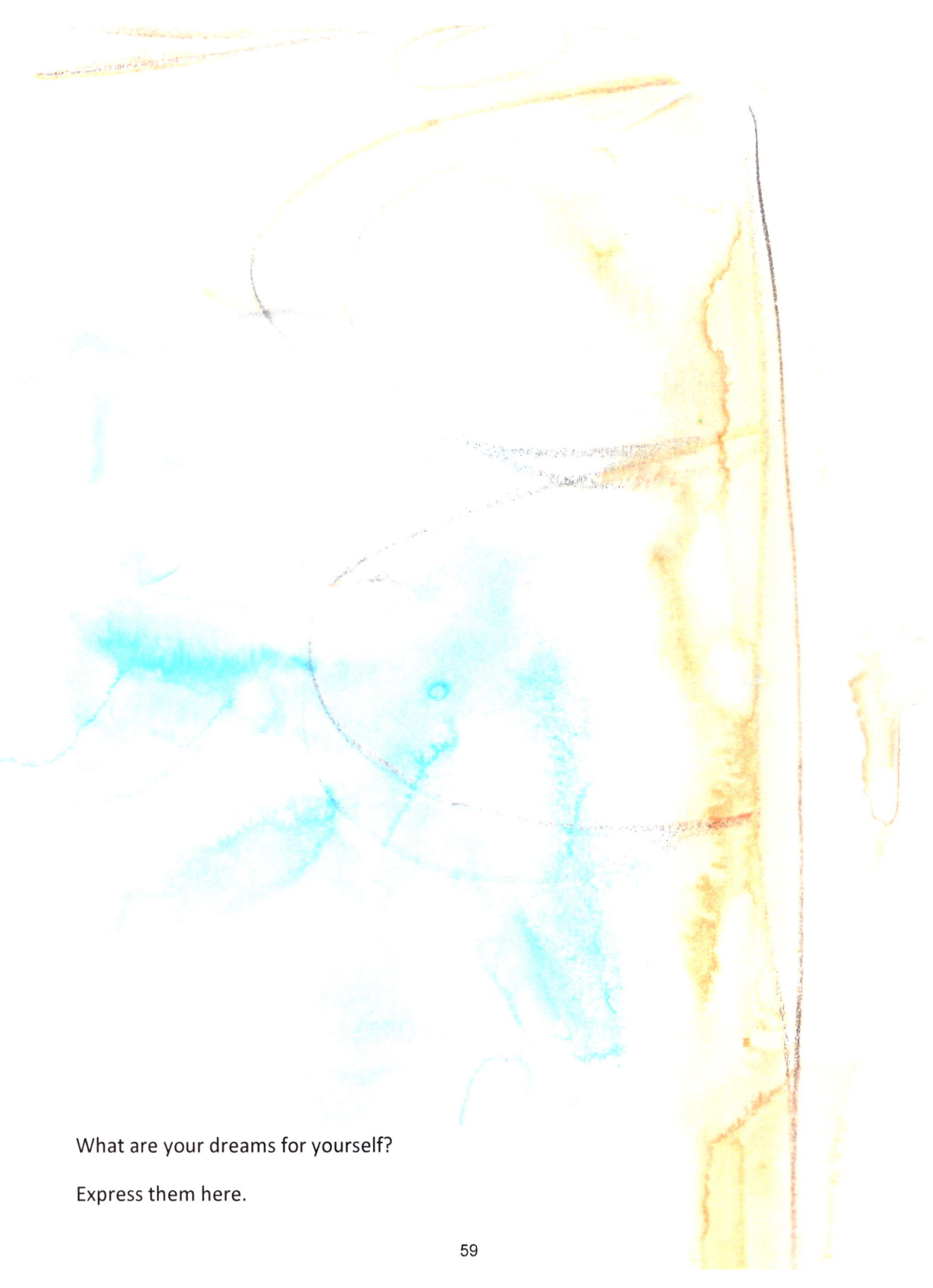

What are your dreams for yourself?

Express them here.

About Me:

I was born in Mountain View California in 1963. Growing up, I don't remember not making things. I had a fabulously creative extended family and they were a big influence. My first job out of high school was as a seamstress and fabric cutter for a pizza restaurant chain with robotic characters. I still dislike fake fur, lol. Over the years I have been a licensed dispensing optician, optical lab tech, owner and provider of my own daycare business, retail sales clerk, merchandiser, resident artist and crafter at a local gift shop, written websites, maid and so many other things.

My true love though is art. Let me tell you a little bit about my creative journey. I can knit, crochet, sew and embroider along with other various arts and crafts. Almost every art form you can find in your local craft shop I have tried. My one true love though was always drawing and painting. Even as a child my mother will tell you that the one way to get me to focus and concentrate was to give me some paper and a pencil.

As an adult I have decided to focus on those creative pursuits I love and let the rest go. My journey to painting and mixed media started with an introduction to the art form by a friend. This was quickly followed by classes from some great teachers like Flora Bowley, Traci Bautista and Pauline Agnew.

I have discovered throughout my artistic journey that I enjoy creating beautiful and unique pieces. These pieces of my art can be very expressive, dark, abstract, or even fluid. I love it when I can share the process and encourage others to follow their creative dreams. As an artist and teacher, I find no greater joy then to see my fellow creatives express their inner soul.

Art is a great healer, a fabulous focus, and rewarding pursuit. I look forward to many adventures in art and hope you all choose to join me!

www.ingramcontent.com/pod-product-compliance
Lightning Source LLC
Chambersburg PA
CBHW050756180526
45159CB00003B/1475